A SHARE OF SUCCESS

A Share of Success

Peter Scudamore and Alan Lee

Foreword by John Francome

STANLEY PAUL
London Melbourne Sydney Auckland Johannesburg

Stanley Paul & Co. Ltd

An imprint of the Hutchinson Publishing Group

17–21 Conway Street, London W1P 6JD

Hutchinson Group (Australia) Pty Ltd
30–32 Cremorne Street, Richmond South, Victoria 3121
PO Box 151, Broadway, New South Wales 2007

Hutchinson Group (NZ) Ltd
32–34 View Road, PO Box 40–086, Glenfield, Auckland 10

Hutchinson Group (SA) Pty Ltd
PO Box 337, Bergvlei 2012, South Africa

First published 1983
© Peter Scudamore and Alan Lee 1983
Set in Linotron Baskerville by
Input Typesetting Ltd, London SW19 8DR

Printed in Great Britain by The Anchor Press Ltd
and bound by Wm Brendon & Son Ltd,
both of Tiptree, Essex

ISBN 0 09 151360 X

Contents

Photographic acknowledgements

For permission to reproduce photographs included in this book, the publisher and authors would like to thank Joan F. Cooke, PA Reuter Photos Ltd, Paddock Studios, Bernard Parkin, Portman Press Bureau Ltd, Provincial Press Agency, Sport and General Press Agency Ltd and Barry Swaebe.

Foreword

by John Francome

National Hunt racing may not quite have the corinthian outlook of days gone by but I like to think it is still one of the few sports in which friendship and fellowship play an important role. It was this which influenced me in April 1982, when Peter Scudamore broke his arm at Southwell and I suddenly found myself back in with a chance of retaining my title as champion jockey.

I was twenty winners behind Scu, the season had six weeks to run and by spending just a few minutes on the equation I realized I had a chance, if a slim one, of overtaking him.

I have heard many people since express astonishment at my decision to quit for the season if and when I drew level, so that Peter and I could share the championship. All I can say is that those people must place too little store in sportsmanship.

Peter had done so well for two seasons that it would have been cruel for him to lose all touch with the prize. Racing is a hard game, as well I know, and maybe I did show a soft side incongruous with the profession. But I have never regretted it for one moment, and I will tell you why.

Jump racing is full of characters – most of them marvellous, warm people with a rich sense of humour and a willingness to give their last penny if your need is greater than theirs. They do not come much better than Michael Scudamore, Peter's father and a man I have admired and respected throughout my time in the sport.

He epitomizes all that is best in racing, and the breeding has produced a similar type in his son.

The first day I saw Peter ride, I was struck by his style and driving commitment to win – and I did not even know who he was at the time. When I came to know him it was not long before I realized he would soon be a real challenger to the best and most successful jockeys in the business. In that, he was doing me a favour.

No winner is easy, no title simply attained, but I had tasted such success over half a decade and more that I needed a new incentive to give of my best. Scu, solemn and determined to dislodge me as champion, gave me that incentive, and managed to do it in a way which endeared him to me and many others in the sport.

I often used to think him too serious, and told him frequently that he should try laughing more. He was quite unlike me in that sense, but it was this single-minded concentration on his job which made him successful. He relaxes more now, confident in his position – but it has not made him any less formidable an opponent.

We often share a bench in the weighing room these days, and spend the periods between races swapping jokes or horror stories about yesterday's falls and today's fears. There is a bond of respect between us, and if I take the mickey out of him mercilessly at times, he knows it is just my way.

Not that we have always been so matey. Our proximity in terms of winners, and our stables' great rivalry, has brought some tense moments on tracks around the country and, more than once, we have exchanged angry words afterwards. It would be amazing if we had not, though, and neither of us remembers, or bears grudges, the following day.

Scu unwittingly forced me into the most hectic month of my racing life last year as I fought to hang on to my title. I made it, just, and we are joint champions throughout 1982–83. Whatever happens this year or next, I am certain of one thing – Peter will be champion in his own right before too long.

1

An Eye for a Horse

It has frequently been said that Peter Scudamore is the best-bred jockey to appear for many years and certainly, with a father who won both the Grand National and the Cheltenham Gold Cup before reluctantly switching to training, his pedigree cannot be faulted.

Michael Scudamore was born in 1932 and has always lived in that section of Britain where England seems to have ended and Wales has not quite begun, a green and pleasant land, rich in farming potential and populated, it often seems, more thickly by animals than humans. He grew up among horses and, like Peter a generation later, was captivated by the notion of riding them for a living, although in Michael's case farming was kept constantly on tap as a standby option.

He rode in a point-to-point at the age of fourteen and did not have long to wait before graduating to the racecourse. For very different reasons, one pleasant, one painful, Michael has a vivid recall of his first and his last rides: 'Back in the forties no one needed a licence to ride as an amateur, and my first mount came by accident. I had gone to Hereford races with my father, who left me watching from the stands while he went off to talk to some pals. Some while later he returned, fetched me down and told me I could ride a spare horse in the hunter chase. There was no time to get nervous; I was hurried off into the weighing room, where the valets fixed me up with some tack, and I was away before I knew it.'

Michael, who had only a dozen rides on the flat before his weight forced him to switch to National Hunt racing, achieved his first jumping winner in the 1948–49 season, on Wild Honey at Chepstow. In the twenty years following that chance debut at Hereford he had about 4000 rides. Exactly 500 of them were winners, and Michael reflects that about the same number fell, though none so disastrously or, in career terms, terminally, as his last.

'It was 1 November 1966. I doubt if I shall ever forget that date. At thirty-four I suppose a lot of jockeys are thinking of giving up anyway, but I had come through a few bad years, when I thought hard about my future, and I was enjoying riding as much as ever before. I had topped forty winners in each of the two previous seasons, and I had ridden another eight in the first couple of months of this one, so I was going quite nicely.

'There was nothing special about the meeting – just a very ordinary mid-week jumps fixture at Wolverhampton, an unlovely sort of course set under some railway arches behind a housing estate. Not a grand place to finish, nor was it the type of accident I could ever have envisaged. After all those rides, all those obstacles, and surviving so many orthodox falls, the one which finished me was a complete freak. My horse slipped up on the flat and just dumped me on the floor in the path of the rest of the field. I took two pretty fierce kicks, one in the chest, the other in the face. I saw stars, but never lost consciousness, just lay there feeling dreadful until the ambulance arrived.

'I remember having to sit up on the stretcher because I was afraid I might choke on the blood that was pouring from my mouth. I could not see much out of my left eye, but at the time I did not dwell on that, just assumed it would clear. But it never did.'

Michael's horrifying injuries included a punctured lung, a jaw broken in two places and disfigurement of his features which neither time nor surgery would ever completely reverse.

'The surgeon put my face together again like a jigsaw at Wolverhampton hospital, but when the doctor broke it to me that I would lose the sight of that eye, I simply would not believe him at first. I told him that I could still see, even if it was a bit blurred, but he explained that the nerve attached to the eye was dead and that within six weeks virtually all the sight I still possessed would disappear. He was beginning to make himself clear. I would never be able to ride again. Everything else would mend, he assured me, but not the eye. And it was quite obvious that I could not race-ride with one eye, as any flying mud could quickly have made me completely blind and a danger to every other jockey as well as myself.

'My first thought was that I would never jump Becher's again. Aintree meant that much to me. I looked forward to the annual pilgrimage for the National meeting as a kid looks forward to Christmas. There was a magic about the place, about the atmosphere . . . there always had been. My life's ambition, right back in schooldays, had been to win the Grand National, and the fact that I had achieved that aim did not mean I was content to stop

'Riding Oxo to victory in 1959 was the highlight of my career – it even beat winning the Gold Cup, I think – but I have good memories of so many other years there. I had sixteen consecutive National rides, which I am told is a record. I got round five times, and finished second and third as well as winning once. Every year, as that first week of April approached, I got a few butterflies, but the adrenaline was really flowing. It was hard to accept that those days were gone.'

But accept it he did and while Mary, his wife of nine years, may well have drawn a long sigh of relief, Michael had to come to terms with his future. He decided that he was out of touch with farming, despite having eighty-four acres of land attached to his home at Hoarwithy, so against his instincts he launched into a new career as a trainer.

At the time of writing his racing life extends to thirty-five years and a great deal has changed under his gaze. Fences, he says, were stiffer and straighter when he was riding – 'You had to be more of a horseman and make the horses jump properly or you would end up on the deck rather a lot' – and safety standards have improved immeasurably over the years. 'The formation of the Jockeys' Association in the early sixties brought about a great many changes. Precautions and services on the courses were improved, and new, stronger helmets were produced for the jockeys. When I started we wore helmets, but they were far smaller and skimpier than those you see today. Goggles were another advance. We never wore them at all in the fifties, and even towards the end of my career we only put them on when the mud was flying; we were scared of getting an eyeful of Perspex if we got kicked. But the jockeys of today wear them all the time, and on balance they are probably right.

'Types of horses which go jumping have altered too, over the years. In the past no lightly boned horses were considered suitable, which meant that not many graduated from the flat to the jump. But nowadays very few are thought too light, and dozens move across from the flat every year.

'The most striking changes have been in the lifestyle of the jockeys. Take travelling for one thing. There were no motorways at all for us to race up and down, which meant it just wasn't practical to try to drive home each night after racing. Early in the season, when most of the meetings take place in the West Country, we would stay down in Torquay, enjoying a bit of a holiday and riding at about three meetings each week. But in the winter, when one could have to go anywhere to ride, each week needed a good deal of planning. I remember during petrol rationing that I often seemed to leave home on Monday or Tuesday morning and not get back until Saturday night.

'Generally, I would arrange to stay with other jockeys and trainers in the locality of the next meeting, but whenever I went to London I stayed at the Savoy Baths in Jermyn Street, just off Piccadilly on the St James's side. It was cheap, at 30s a night, and I had a lot of fun there.

'I always thought a homeless jockey could have lived at the Savoy quite happily over a long period. There was everything on hand for the single bloke. It was right behind Fortnum and Mason, for one thing, and just over the road was the best cheese shop I've ever seen. Just

12

up an alleyway, there was a clothes shop where I often used to buy a shirt, and for eating and drinking it was difficult to think of a better area.

'The bar we jockeys used to patronize was called Eileen's. The landlady always gave us a welcome, and we knew there was a drink available at most hours. Directly opposite was Wheelers, the fish restaurant, and the staff there knew us all on Christian-name terms, too. Our fish would be specially prepared – no fatty sauces of course – but despite the usual protestations, we usually found a bottle of Chablis stuck in front of us, and that meant an extra hour in the sauna back at the Savoy.

'Plenty of jockeys overdid the evenings out in London, of course, and I remember at least one occasion when a couple of lads turned up at the Saturday meeting in their dinner jackets. I was no angel, but I had to be fairly careful because I was always wasting to get down even to 10 stone 5 or 6. There was no point in having a good night out then putting up so much overweight the next day that you lost rides over it.

'All sorts turned up at the Savoy, from famous politicians down to common tramps, and now and again it did get a bit lively. Rugby internationals always brought a crowd in, and I remember the police being called in more than once the night before a Twickenham match.

'I often went there with Arthur Freeman, another jockey, and we usually stayed in the "Royal suite". At least, we called it that, but in fact it was just a couple of bunks in the corner. That's all the accommodation was, just bunks curtained off – rows of them on three different floors. But, if you had enjoyed a drink, a meal and a sweat in the sauna, that was all you wanted.

'Arthur and I usually went up to Fortnum's for a coffee or a glass of milk in the mornings before driving to racing, and there was a girl among the waitresses that Arthur really took a fancy to. He ended up marrying her.

'The great thing about the Savoy was that I always met some pals there. I could walk in by myself, go up to the reception desk and be greeted as an old friend, then find that three or four other jockeys were in that night too. And I would always know where to find them – at Eileen's or Wheelers.

'For most jockeys, there has been little need to stay in London since the coming of motorways, and the Savoy went out of fashion as a racing hotel. It closed down three or four years ago, I believe, and a lot of people mourned its passing. Full of memories, that place.'

Michael, one suspects, regrets the changes of pace and emphasis in the jockeys' lifestyle which have brought down the curtain on such social days. He is not one to indulge in the embittered moans of 'it's not the same as in my day' which the idle bystander can detect in racing as in every other sport. But, beneath the surface, he may privately be glad that he rode in his own era and not in the more hectic environment which his son so relishes.

'Peter and I have often discussed this. My own view is simply that the jockeys' job has become more professional – and I am talking about jump jockeys, not the flat boys whose lives have been surrounded by commercialism for years. Without wishing to be derogatory to my own generation, I feel jockeys are generally better educated these days, and their outlook is different from how I remember mine to have been.

'We used to live for today. Bugger tomorrow – that could take care of itself. But Peter and his generation are rightly more concerned about their futures, and I think the influence of the Jockeys' Association is pretty strong in this regard.

'As to the purely social aspects of the life, I would not claim that the jockeys of today don't enjoy themselves – Peter would never forgive me. But I think it is a fact that many of them marry younger these days, and understandably don't stop out as long as we did after racing. It was part of the pleasure of the job to us; on a Saturday night, with no racing the following day, we would probably make several stops on the way home and not clock in until pretty late, with a good few drinks inside us. Maybe the breathalyser has helped put a stop to that. No jockey can afford to lose his driving licence.'

A year after Michael and Mary moved into the picturesque old house where they have spent all their married days, Peter was born. Their daughter Nicky arrived two years later and both have been brought up with horses as their closest friends and neighbours. In the last years of Michael's riding career he went to Scandinavia each summer to ride, taking the children with him. 'It was good experience for me and a broadening sort of holiday for them. They have both been back since, using the contacts I made to ride,' he reflects.

A short man with comfortably craggy features and a warm manner, Michael is honest and analytical about the progress of his son in the racing game. 'He always used to cry as a baby,' he says. 'A restless sort. And he has remained restless and ambitious ever since. Often he has been too impatient to reach for standards and goals, but then maybe that is a good fault.

'We often used to argue about what he should ride and what he should not. Left to him, he would have accepted anything, but he had to learn that some animals were going to do him no good, and might well do him a lot of harm. Mary still gets upset now when he rides bad horses, and in the early days she was even more critical. I remember when Peter rode his first point-to-point winner, we were all watching from a bank – Mary, the horse's owner, called Herbie, and myself. I am relatively impassive during a race, but Mary and Herbie were marching up and down the bank in opposite directions, each oblivious to the other, both looking frantic with worry.

'Peter has had good opportunities which everyone needs if they are to get to the top. But I don't think he has been smiled upon because of my name. He just happens to have been in the right place at the right time. Take his first winner, and the story behind it. . . .

'In 1978 there was heavy snow in our parts during the spring. We had been virtually cut off for days, and there was no racing. It was as much as we could do to keep the horses in the yard fed and watered. One morning at nine o'clock, Peter and I were in the yard when the phone rang. It was Lionel Ensten, who had owned one of the finest 2-mile chasers I ever rode, a horse named

Greek Town. He said he wanted Peter to ride for him in a point-to-point that afternoon at Cottenham in Cambridgeshire. I thought he was joking, as everything was blanketed with white outside our window, but Lionel assured me that the meeting was definitely on, so after a bit of thought and some discussion we agreed to go.

'For some way I still thought it was a fool's errand, but gradually the covering of snow became lighter, and although it was still lying on the ground at St Neots, there was none at all at Cottenham and Lionel was right – the meeting was on. One of the first people we saw was Toby Balding, who had apparently come to watch a horse run with a view to buying him. But later in the afternoon, after Peter had ridden, Toby came up to me again and had clearly had a close look at Peter's riding ability. "He's got more style than you ever had," he told me. I was to remember that, because some time later – at the start of the following season, in fact – Toby phoned up and said, "What weight can that streak of a son of yours do?" He wanted him to ride Rolyat in an amateurs' race at Devon – but if we had not battled through the snow to Cottenham, Peter would never have got the ride.

'Even then, we were doubtful whether he would make it to Devon on the appointed day. He was driving an old red car, which is still parked round the back of my yard now. It was not very reliable, and although it had got him to Fontwell Park the previous day, we thought the cross-country trip to Devon might be too much for it. But it got there, and Peter rode his first winner.

'It was that same year that Peter went to Stow, for an estate agent's job. Mary's father was an auctioneer, so it seemed a fairly natural progression, but I always knew that Peter was not too keen on the idea and that he probably wouldn't have gone at all unless we allowed him to keep a close contact with racing. That was why I arranged for him to ride out with David Nicholson, but I never imagined their link would grow to what it is today. Another fortunate coincidence.

'Peter has learned to make friends easily and adapt quickly to strange situations if they are in his interests, which is all part of the jockey's job. I think his greatest quality on a horse is the ability to switch his mount off and leave him totally relaxed. Yet when he is not riding Peter seldom relaxes himself. He can be very intense, and if things are not going well it is easy to imagine the end of the world is only a few minutes away.

'I can see many reasons for his success in his attitude at home. Although he can sleep anywhere, which is of great value in his lifestyle, everyone has to know when he is awake. He is never satisfied with himself, and is always willing to learn something new if he thinks it will help his riding. Above all, cliché or not, he has tremendous ambition and a great will to win. If he ever lost that, he would lose much of his success.'

2

In Father's Footsteps

The morning after the Grand National of 1959, many national newspapers carried a cosy family photograph of the winning jockey bouncing his nine-month-old son on his shoulders. As is customary on such occasions, father was asked if son would follow in his footsteps. 'I don't know if he will become a jockey,' came the reply, 'but I'll certainly buy him his first pony to help.'

A pony was duly bought, encouragement given and gratefully received, and twenty-three years after that homely picture appeared, the son's photograph, of a slightly later vintage, was kept permanently handy in newspaper offices. Not only had he followed in father's footsteps but in spring of 1982 he had achieved a family first and become joint champion jockey.

The pale face and searching eyes of Peter Scudamore were now familiar, if not famous, features. His rise to prominence in the precarious world of National Hunt racing had been startling by any standards, and for two seasons he had been engaged in a virtually constant head-to-head battle with John Francome for the jockeys' title. Francome, his handsome head of Wiltshire curls driven to new degrees of motivation by the young pretender to his domain, had won the first contest, and the second had finished level; the sagas behind both might have been scripted for maximum tension.

Father Michael Scudamore still looked on, privately more proud than his public demeanour admitted. His own riding days had long since gone, ended by his hideous, freakish fall, and now he trained a small string of horses and farmed on the Welsh borders in the sort of idyllically pastoral surroundings that would do credit to an advert for Irish butter. It was there, in a farmhouse dating back to the sixteenth century, that Peter grew up.

It may sound fancifully romantic to claim that the boy had always dreamed of being champion jockey but, according to Peter and all those close to him, that really was the case. Michael tells an apt out-of-school tale. 'When Peter was about eight or nine he had to write an essay entitled something like "Twenty Years Hence". He started it with the sentence, "I have been champion jockey for the past five seasons. . . ." '

But if Peter, even then in short trousers, was single-minded about his future, others in his family were less convinced it was quite such a good idea. Not that they had anything against racing; far from it, the sport was in the blood of them all. But were the risks encountered daily by a jump jockey rendered worthwhile by the job's rewards? Hence, there was a difference of opinion.

Peter's grandfather, Geoffrey Scudamore, a man with a kindly, ruddy face and a contented reminiscing manner, was an example of those who voted against. He had ridden to hounds throughout his younger life, rode under rules as an amateur and went on to train National Hunt horses. His most auspicious success was to train the winner of the 1956 Triumph Hurdle at Cheltenham – a horse named Square Dance, ridden by his son Michael. His other, less celebrated memories up to his death in December 1982 included having ridden three different ways around his local Hereford course, which seems to have undergone a good deal of redesigning, and to have won three times in eight days with one particular horse, each time on a course which has since become extinct. He recalled, 'It was a reliable old 3-mile chaser called Sawfish owned by Wilfred Tate, father of the current trainer, Martin Tate. We ran him at Wye, in Kent, then on the old course, Colwell Park, Malvern, and lastly down at Buckfastleigh in Devon, and he won the lot. There were no four-day declarations in those days, and the bookies never caught up with the horse, so it was a very successful week. Seems funny, looking back on it . . . there was no time to go home in between the races, we were on the road all the time. A car and a two-wheel trailer wobbling along behind. We stopped at pubs for bread and cheese, then headed on to the next racecourse. It was hectic, but you couldn't have complained if a few more weeks had been like it.'

Despite such colourful exploits, Geoffrey's primary business was farming 350 acres of good Herefordshire land, and it was in this direction that he was anxious to point his grandson. He failed graciously, and in July 1982, as I sat with the three generations of Scudamore menfolk watching Worcestershire play cricket on Hereford racecourse, his grandfather mischievously chided Peter over his obsessive thumbing through racing form-books but, I suspect, felt far from malevolent in the light of Peter's achievements to date.

The other opposition to a career in the saddle came from Peter's mother Mary. One look at her pedigree and this too is surprising, for when she married Michael, as Mary Duffield, in 1957 she was known as a keen and capable horsewoman. Peter was born a year later, and the family snaps confirm the guess that he was sitting on a horse before he was walking.

It was Mary who taught Peter to ride, as she remembers now. 'Mike was always away racing, so it was the natural thing for me to do. Pete was very small when he had his first pony. He was called Daisy, and every time he put his head down to eat some grass, Peter slid down his neck and fell off. As he grew bigger though, he took quite easily to riding, and I shall never forget the day we went to look at another pony for him.

'Walter Biddlecombe, Terry's father, had contacted us and said he had one for sale, called Black Opal. We went over to his place to have a look and he invited Peter to get on and ride the pony. "Why not pop him over this fence?" he said, and it looked a low, harmless obstacle, so he did. Gradually, Walter kept putting the level up and slowly I began to panic. Peter had never jumped anything that high before and I thought he must come off. But the pony was a marvellous jumper, and Peter stayed on. We bought him straight away.

'That pony was perfect for Peter, but he gave us some

20

headaches. He was never one to settle for being penned in, and often used to jump over our gates and get free during the night. But he seldom went very far. Usually, the lads would find him lying in the road the next morning, fast asleep.

'I think he played games with us sometimes. If we were going racing, we went over to the fields to bring him into his box. Often, he would run away and refuse to be caught, but more than once we had given up and walked back to the house, only to find he had beaten us to it and was waiting patiently to go into his stable.

'We lost him for a week once. It was the usual thing, disappearing during the night, only this time he was nowhere to be found the following morning. As the days passed we had virtually lost all hope, and naturally the children were very upset. But a week later we had a phone call from a farmer to say he had him. He lived seven miles away!'

But although Mary encouraged Peter to ride, she was far more negative when it came to racing. To be blunt, she simply did not want Peter to be a jockey and suggested any number of alternative professions in an attempt to divert him.

Michael explains. 'Mary had never shown she was nervous about my riding, and I think I can understand why. When we met, I had been a jockey for a number of years and gave the impression that I could look after myself. There was also nothing she could have done to stop me, even if she had wanted to. But with Peter it was different. Mary had a chance to find him something else to do, away from the obvious dangers of the jumping game before he even started. So she tried. She will say she never actively discouraged him from racing, but certainly she never encouraged him.'

Even Michael, who must have craved for Peter the same life which gave him so much pleasure, never thought to push his son into the jockey's world. 'I just wanted him to enjoy life and be a success at whatever he made up his mind to do. If he did decide to be a jockey, and if we are honest that was always the most natural thing for him to do, then it was vital that he made a go of it. The worst thing of all, in my view, would have been for him to end up as a spare-ride jockey, scraping a living from the sport and with nothing else to turn to.'

With that in mind, Peter's parents tried to ensure that he always would have an alternative. Education, they agreed, was vital. Peter first went to the village primary school near their home in Hoarwithy, then to junior school in Hereford and on to a prep school across the border in Wales. Finally, he graduated to Belmont Abbey public school, where he stayed until the age of eighteen, becoming deputy head boy.

Peter confesses to having felt frustrated by his years at school. 'I kept home and school entirely separate in my mind. During holidays I never talked about school, seldom thought about it and did very little work. At the time, I just didn't appreciate the benefits I was reaping from school.

'I never thought of myself as being at all bright, but I did have the capacity to work hard when I needed to, such as when exams were drawing near. I stayed on to take my A-levels, and I don't regret that for a moment. I only took two instead of three and opted for a pair of rather obscure subjects – medieval history and British constitution – mainly because some of my friends were doing the same. It taught me to buckle down and work to a specific end, and I believe it matured me. But I can't honestly say I enjoyed it.'

By the time he left school Peter was already well versed in the workings of a stable yard. His father had been training since 1967 and Peter had grown up in Utopia, able to help out whenever the urge took him, without the responsibility of set duties.

'I must have been very disliked in the yard,' he says. 'I did my two horses from the age of ten, but no one could really discipline me. Life was all a great game at the time, and if anything went wrong I could always run to mother. The head lad, Philip Turner, is still there now, but I wonder how he survived my behaviour. I think he found me impossible to cope with. I was always up to tricks.'

Michael has a different anecdote from those apparently far-off days. 'Peter was a great legpuller around the yard and had a good sense of humour. He also appeared to be quite fearless. When he was twelve a horse bolted with him. It raced off through the meadow and down into the stream. We were all panicking, but Peter had a big grin on his face and yelled at us "Look, no brakes."

'He worked his hours in the yard and, I suppose, would like to have spent more of his time there. But one thing we did insist on was his education. Mary was always better at disciplining him than I was. In some ways I think he took more notice of her.'

But Peter recalls, 'Both Nicky and I had great respect for father. He never hit us and seldom lost his temper but on those occasions he did put his foot down we never went against him.'

While Mary still harboured hopes of diverting Peter's interests elsewhere, Michael accepted the likelihood that he would end up in racing, and set about ensuring that he took the safest, most sensible route.

'He had made up his mind, I knew that, so I wanted it for him because he wanted it for himself. If he had said he wanted to race cars or motorbikes then I would have dissuaded him, because they are easy ways to the graveyard. But at least with horses I had been through it all myself and could advise him.

'Peter went hunting with the Ross Harriers, which was good experience and in itself an education in horsemanship. But he was always impatient to do more, and pestered me endlessly to let him ride in point-to-points. Often I refused because, to my mind, point-to-pointing is far more dangerous than riding under rules. The horses are often unreliable, there are too many runners for the size of the course and some of the riders have very little idea.

'It was hard work convincing Peter. He was strong-minded even then, and although he would usually admit afterwards that he had been wrong about something, he did it reluctantly.

'He left home once. He was sixteen at the time and

we had argued as usual, about a forthcoming point-to-point. He knew he could ride a certain horse in one of the races and I knew the thing was a beast and very likely to bury him. But this time he didn't relent and threatened to walk out unless we changed our minds. We stood firm, so he packed his clothes into a bag and left. It was tempting to try to stop him, but instead I let him go. About twenty minutes later I got in the car and drove off in the direction I knew he would have headed. He was on the side of the road, having second thoughts. I picked him up and took him to a pub, where we sat in a corner and talked the thing out. Eventually, although he may not have agreed with my thinking, he at least accepted it.'

For Peter that day was a turning point. He lost the battle over that point-to-point race, but he was now winning the war over his future.

'It was still worthwhile trying to turn his mind to things other than racing occasionally, if only as an exercise. A good opportunity arose one day when I saw in the paper that the jockey, John Harty, had been called to the bar. "There you are," I told Peter. "It's clear you should get a profession behind you before you get too deep into racing." He walked away, saying nothing, but came back in the room a few minutes later looking extremely melancholy, and moaned, "I haven't got the brains for that – all I want to be is a jockey".'

Peter had two rides on the flat for his father and then, at eighteen, with his A-levels behind him, both passed, he went to spend a summer working for trainer Willie Stephenson at his Royston yard. A happy coincidence this, as Michael Scudamore had ridden Stephenson's horses for many years, most memorably when piloting Oxo to victory in the 1959 National. Stephenson was also the uncle of David Nicholson, a fact which was later to have an influence on young Scudamore's career.

Peter's memories of that summer are sharp and warm. 'It was something I wanted to do, partly to see for myself if I was suited to stable life away from my home environment. This time there was no opposition from my mother or father – in mother's case, I think she was convinced

I would be worked so hard in the yard that it would put me off for life. She was right about the work, which was very strenuous, but wrong about the effect it would have on me. I enjoyed it to the extent that it increased my determination to find a future in racing.

'I stayed at Willie's house and learned a great deal from just watching and listening to this experienced trainer work. I was expected to be in the yard at six each morning and again in the evening, riding out every day and doing my share of the chores around Willie's farms. In the afternoons we would often go out on to the farm and chase cattle, in the useful sense.

'But, as it turned out, even Willie Stephenson saw my future rather differently from my own views. He told me I should not be a jockey, which came as a surprise, and he was actually responsible for getting me the only job outside racing I have ever had.

'One lunchtime we had just finished work when he told me there was a man he wanted me to meet. I was to smarten myself up and report to the Bull, a pub in the town. There, he introduced me to someone called Michael Haydon, who turned out to be a partner in a large estate agent's business. "This is Peter Scudamore and he is coming to work for you next year," said Willie, suggesting he knew Mr Haydon rather well. Although slightly taken aback, the estate agent conceded that there would be a vacancy in his office at Stow-on-the-Wold in about six months' time and he would certainly consider me for the job.

'My view of all this was fairly phlegmatic. I reasoned that it was six months distant and I would avoid it when I had to. In the meantime, I was enjoying the chance to race-ride from time to time.

'Willie gave me a ride over hurdles at Kempton on a little horse called Force Ten. I finished fourth and came back to unsaddle feeling fairly pleased with myself. But Willie, in a nice, roundabout way, implied that if Peter Greenall had been riding, the horse would probably have won. I was very deflated, because at the time I considered myself to be at least as good as Lester Piggott and Terry Biddlecombe rolled into one. But I am certain now that it did me good – Willie probably even said it deliberately to put me down. He was a very shrewd man and in my time with him I learned a fair bit about the world outside racing, and came away knowing that life was not quite as easy as I had imagined.

'I thought I was in for my first winner when I rode Smidley Hill, which was owned by friends of our family, Gwyn and Barbara Davies, who still have horses with my father now. It was at Newton Abbot and only my second ride over hurdles. We jumped the second last flight three or four lengths clear and with no apparent danger. But the horse broke down going to the last, and that was another lesson learned: nothing in racing can be taken for granted.

'When I went home after my time at Willie Stephenson's I completely forgot about the estate agents' job, and it came as quite a shock when Michael Haydon phoned up one day and invited me for an interview. It would have been disrespectful and ungrateful of me to back out at that stage, and my pride then took over. If I was to be considered, then I meant to get the job.

'It was partly to prove to my mother that I could do other things. She was still for ever telling me I was stupid to consider riding for a living, and that as I had A-levels I should use them in a profession. She annoyed me sometimes, and I never was going to come round to her way of thinking. But at least the job was a compromise. I was duly appointed, but not required for a few months, so in the meantime I broadened my racing knowledge and worldliness a little more by going to Norway for a couple of months. This was a holiday with a bit of work attached. I rode out for Dennis Holmberg, one of the best trainers over there, and had some rides for him. I saw a lot of the country and grew to like it; I was to return many times in the years to follow.

'I am willing to admit I had an inflated opinion of my own ability at that time. Both in Willie Stephenson's yard and in Norway I was cocky, believing I was far better than I could possibly be. I expect I was unpopular – it is the kind of thing one never knows at the time –

but with a famous name and a big head, I can't see any way I can have been liked much by the lads in the yards.

'Every time I had a ride I was striving to make an impression. There is nothing wrong with that, of course, but I was also oblivious to advice, considering my own half-baked theories to be superior.

'My first ride over hurdles in Norway was an education. I had noticed that the Scandinavians rode in a different style from that which I was used to, allowing their horses to run virtually through the small hurdles, rather than kicking them to jump. Foolishly, I took no notice and failed to adapt my style. I was riding a Polish-bred horse called Da Gol, and set off in my usual, English-orientated style. Approaching the third, I kicked the horse into it and we took off three strides out, hitting the top of the hurdle hard and coming down heavily. As I returned ruefully to the weighing room I was met by one of the stewards, a Norwegian woman, who pointed out – no doubt with good intentions – that it was wrong to kick horses into the obstacles on Scandinavian tracks. I replied scornfully that it was the only way to ride. "You will learn," she said rather condescendingly. But she was right, I did.

'A short while before starting work for Bernard Thorpe, the estate agents, I went with my father to the Foxhunters meeting at Cheltenham. David Nicholson was there, and father – who knew him very well – asked if I could ride out for him while I was working at Stow, as his yard was only a mile or so from the office. David agreed readily, and I later learned that father had planned this because he feared I would never stick at the job otherwise. But, ironically, although the arrangement kept me working for a time, it eventually led to my leaving.

'My heart was never in the property business. At least, it was never in the job I was assigned, for the simple reason that I had no incentive and very little responsibility. I could see no future in it for me, so my ambition to do things well evaporated.

'Just occasionally I was sent out on something which

did grab my interest, and then I really tried. Looking at houses for measuring was quite a challenge, and looking at farms in a surveying role was also an attractive if rather rare diversion. But for the most part my duties were those of an office boy, doing the common clerical work and going out to put up signs. I was absolutely hopeless at showing people round houses because my lack of enthusiasm and salesmanship must have been transparent, and I expect I put off more potential buyers than I attracted.

'Fortunately, my bosses were obliging about my desire to split my time. Each morning I went to David Nicholson's yard to ride out, and now I found I was picking up some rides elsewhere. I scored my first winner over hurdles on Toby Balding's old horse Rolyat in a 3-mile race at Devon and Exeter.'

The Sporting Life's close-up guide to that race, an amateur riders' handicap hurdle on 31 August 1978, reveals that Rolyat started at 11–4, second in the betting to the odds-on mount of that well-known amateur, Mr Jim Wilson. It also reports that Rolyat 'chased leader from second till went on 7th, soon clear, hit last, unchallenged', which sounds comfortable enough. But Peter recalls, 'The horse did not seem to like the Devon start, which for 3-mile races is down a chute separate from the actual course, and as the tapes went up he whipped round and I thought all was lost. He only settled after the second, but from then on I was confident we would win.'

Soon afterwards Scudamore rode his first chase winner, on John Yardley's Majestic Touch at Ludlow, and in all he collected seven winners that season, frequently deputizing on David Nicholson's horses when his regular jockeys were absent injured.

'My good luck was the misfortune of two others. Roy Mangan had been badly hurt in a fall and Jeff King, who was riding the majority of David's horses at the time, broke his leg. The yard had been afflicted by the cough until Christmas and when things started moving again I was on their first winner, Jacko.

'The Aintree meeting gave me a particularly memorable win. Mac's Chariot was the horse which had broken Jeff's leg and was not an easy ride, having fallen regularly in recent outings. But I got him round and beat Royal Mail, who was to start favourite for the National three years later.'

That season, like most others in Scudamore's brief but eventful racing life, ended in injury. He was riding a horse called Regal Command at Ascot when a heavy fall left his arm extremely sore. He was sent for an X-ray at Moreton hospital, and it was confirmed that there was a hairline fracture. Not having an adequate casualty unit themselves, Moreton referred him to Cheltenham hospital for a plaster, but by that stage the pain had eased and Scudamore decided he would ignore the advice. 'It seemed okay,' he recalls, 'and I couldn't be bothered to go and sit at another hospital. So I passed myself fit to continue riding, and I was back on board at the next Ascot meeting, a week later. I rode Westbury Lodge in a chase and two fences out I was upsides Ridley Lamb on Another Captain, with a clear chance of winning. I turned my stick to hit the horse down the shoulder and suddenly felt the bone in my arm move. It gave way, quite without warning, and although the pain was nothing like as severe as it had been from the original fall, it was very uncomfortable. I finished the race beaten, and this time there was no choice. I had to go to hospital and subject myself to the plaster. Of course, I should have done so when I was first injured, but impetuosity had got the better of me again.

'I still managed to ride one or two more before the end of the season, including another winner, and the pattern of my life was virtually mapped out on the day David Nicholson asked if I would consider coming to him full-time, as assistant trainer.

'I had no qualms about giving up my job at Stow, but equally I have no regrets about the year I spent there. I saw something outside racing and, heaven forbid, I could always go back to it if the need ever arose.

'But joining David was too good an opportunity to miss. Father was pleased, I think, and even mother was not against the idea. She had probably seen it coming some way off, and managed to lull herself into thinking that if I went as assistant trainer, it would mean I would not be race-riding. By the time she discovered just how wrong an assumption that was, it was far too late to matter.'

3

Horses in the Blood

The light of humour was plain and bright in the eyes of
John Geoffrey Scudamore, but his face was held rigidly
straight as he tackled his grandson on one of his pet
subjects. 'More amateur riders' races on the cards, that's
what we need,' said Geoffrey. 'And a lot more races for
ladies only would be an improvement too.'

When he had first heard these slanderous suggestions,
Peter had reacted irritably. Now, after several such
jousting conversations over the years, he merely smiled
and asked if it was not about time grandfather accepted
that farming was a dying industry?

Margaret, as fluffy and fussing a grandmother as anyone could wish for, giggled in the background and confided that this teasing was all part of the menu whenever
the Scudamores of two generations apart got together.
It was old Geoff's sense of humour, and Peter had
learned to cope and counter.

Such mischief-making, however, led to the speculation
that Geoffrey's initial protestations about Peter's choice
of career had not been too seriously intended. It was not
hard to sense his involvement; several times a week he
phoned Peter to ask about the performances of his rides,
and although he seldom had a bet – 'Peter never gives
me any good things' – he pored contentedly over *The
Sporting Life* in the front room of his charmingly rambling
farmhouse near Hereford.

Geoff's son Handley, Michael's younger brother,
supervises the farming of the 350 acres these days. Until
his death, the senior member of the family was satisfied
with his large and productive vegetable garden, and the

31

ancient, brick-based greenhouse where he spent hours each summer.

When he talked of Peter he was philosophical. 'Whatever I wanted would have made no difference. He always was his own man, and he intended to do just what he wanted in life. And he hasn't made a bad job of it so far, has he?'

Horses, after all, run in the Scudamore blood. Quite how far back, nobody knows. The family tree chart, which lives at Geoffrey's old house and needs a magnifying glass to be read at all, reveals that their origins are Norman and that the early Scudamore settlers in England could thank the Battle of Hastings. There is no evidence of any equine leaning, however, beyond Geoffrey's father, John.

'He was never involved in racing, but he was a marvellous rider, a real horseman,' recalled Geoffrey. 'He showed horses at the highest level, but farming always came first with father. I remember him once saying that the worst thing that could happen to any young farmer was to get a brokendown racehorse on his property. If he got him right and he won once, it would ruin for him life, so father said.'

Geoffrey's racing interests began in the manner you would expect of a Herefordshire farmer, on the point-to-point courses around the county. 'I hunted frequently, always did enjoy that, but I started to get interested in race-riding when I had a very good horse in the local Ross Harriers point-to-point. I won their big race eleven years in succession, although it was not always without incident.

'One year I was cruising in the lead when we fell. But I never let go of the horse and I was able to remount and win easily. Then, another time, I had got down to post when I realized I had forgotten to declare my 3 pounds overweight for a previous win. I told the starter what had happened, then galloped back to the clerk of the scales. He accepted the late declaration all right, and I was just in time for the start. We won again, so all was well.'

It was only natural that a young amateur with such a record between the flags should become popular among trainers, and Geoffrey began to ride under rules for Wilfred Tate during the thirties. His memories are of the small country courses which long ago wound up their operations, of big crowds of chiefly farming folk, of sporting atmosphere and, yes, the occasional good winner.

Sawfish was probably the best horse he rode, and a picture of the partnership still stands in the study of the farmhouse. But despite Geoffrey's self-deprecating claims, he rode plenty more winners and many were provided by Tate.

'He was a hard bugger,' said Geoffrey, a broad smile spreading across his ruddy features. 'Hard but fair. He would often call me on a Thursday evening and say he had two or three horses entered somewhere on the Saturday. I would suggest meeting him at the track, but he always insisted that I went to stay with him on the Friday night so he could keep an eye on me.

'He bought Sawfish for only £4.10s. It should have been £5 but he knocked off ten bob because he said he didn't want the halter. He knew what he was doing.'

It was, however, an oversight by Wilfred Tate which denied Geoffrey the chance of a ride around Aintree's National course. 'I never came close to a ride in the National, I was never of that class, but I was down to ride for Wilfred in the Foxhunters one year. When I got to the course, more than a bit nervous about those fences, I was told I couldn't ride because Wilfred had declared the horse five minutes after the deadline. I didn't know whether I was upset or just relieved.'

With remarkable clarity, Geoffrey remembered the West Country start to each season, the August programme which has progressively thinned out over the years, with the loss of course after course through economic cutbacks. 'We always used to call it the Devon fortnight. We stayed down, of course, and apart from the surviving tracks at Haldon and Newton Abbot, we raced at Buckfastleigh, Totnes, Torquay and Plymouth. There was a meeting about every other day and it was a very friendly way to start the jump season.'

His riding contemporaries were legends such as

33

Frenchie Nicholson and Fulke Walwyn and, although farming remained his full-time occupation and racing an unpaid hobby, he had begun to ride more and more frequently when his jockeyship was shelved with the' onset of war.

Geoffrey joined the RAF, left his home in Panbrook and his two growing sons in the care of Margaret. His home leave was rare, but soon after one such visit had ended, news reached Margaret that he had been shot down over enemy territory. The news came from the Casualty branch of the Air Ministry, couched diplomatically and sympathetically, but leaving the main question unanswered. His plane had 'not been heard from again' following the raid over the Ruhr. Sergeant Scudamore, who had been flying in the Halifax as wireless operator and air gunner, was missing.

In the days which followed, the picture was clarified. The aircraft had gone down with full crew aboard, crash landing on a hilltop. Most of the crew had suffered injuries; Geoffrey's face was badly lacerated and he lost a great deal of blood. But they all survived.

For two years Geoffrey had a new and unwanted home. It was Stalag IVB, Muhlberg-on-Elbe, Saxony, a bunk in a barrack house sardine-packed with 700 prisoners of war.

In a book written ten years after the war ended, Geoff Taylor, a Bomber Command colleague of Geoffrey Scudamore, wrote of his days in IVB. He described how 'It spread across the newly harvested fields, an ugly and alien place in this land of farms and crops, and featureless except for the stilted guard-towers along the wire.' Of the living quarters, Taylor wrote:

The brick-floored, barn-like barrack was almost entirely occupied by rickety wooden bunks; bunks that rose in layers almost to the ceiling; bunks crowded together in tiers of three and blocks of twelve like grotesque, gloomy burlesques of those structures you see toddlers climbing in playgrounds. Down the barrack side opposite the rabbit-warren of bunks . . . there was a narrow strip of brick floor. This area was dominated by two flat-topped smoking stoves connected to a central chimney by crumbling horizontal flues flanked by crude wooden benches. Sagging lines of washing and ranks of cooking utensils, apparently made from old cans, completed the general effect of a thieves' kitchen. But for the absence of blowsy slatterns slopping grog at the benches and a drunken fiddler or two it could have been one of Hogarth's gin-mill scenes of eighteenth-century London come to life.*

Stalag IVB was intended as an army camp, but the overcrowding of all camps operated by the Luftwaffe meant that half of it was apportioned to the Air Force. Geoffrey recalls watching the Army prisoners next door and noting the stark differences in behaviour on the two sides of the fence. 'We were scruffy and rather insubordinate, but the Army boys were sparklingly smart, their boots polished and their uniforms neat. It was their way of showing up the Germans; ours was to try to escape, which for an RAF prisoner was virtually compulsory. I sometimes thought that if an Army prisoner had been offered a jar of coffee or a tin of boot polish, he would probably have taken the polish.

'You got used to the conditions eventually, grew so that you hardly noticed the fact that there was only one wash basin between 700 men and that the camp smelled unpleasantly all the time. But the boredom just got worse, more intense as the weeks and months went past. That was the worst thing, having so much time to do nothing, and think what you might have been doing elsewhere.'

Geoffrey befriended a man named Terry Hunt, the unluckiest prisoner of all. He was a photographer who had joined an RAF command for one mission in pursuance of his job. It happened to be the night they were shot down. But Hunt never lost his camera, nor his desire to take pictures, and between long games of bridge with Geoffrey, he walked the camp with his equipment concealed inside a book.

The photographs he took inside the camp would have gained him a minimum of thirty days in solitary, but he was never discovered, and Geoffrey still had the pictures

* *Piece of Cake* (George Mann, 1956).

35

among his souvenirs when he died. They show the hateful treatment meted out to Russian prisoners, looking like scarecrows and forced to scavenge among discarded food tins for scraps. 'Next to them,' says Geoffrey, 'we were treated very well.

'The Red Cross food parcels kept us going. The Germans barely fed us anything at all, but we learned to make the parcels last. To try to make the conditions more homely, we built shelves in the barrack hut for our food. Now and again the Germans would have a blitz and rip them down, purely out of spite.

'Most of the Germans were open to bribing. Cigarettes were the best blackmail because their ration was small and our supplies, from the Red Cross, relatively large. But coffee went well too.

'The Russians came to relieve us eventually, but even then we were not free. They showed no signs of liberating us, so finally we escaped. It was a pretty hairy operation, across the girders of a broken railway bridge, but we made it to Leipzig and virtually fell into the arms of the Americans. We were all dreaming of steaks, chips and eggs, but instead they fed us on liquid babyfood! It seemed harsh, but it was for our own good. Some people killed themselves by overeating too soon after a spell in a camp.'

When he first stepped on some scales after his release it was to discover that, after years of trying, he was at last a good jockey's weight. 'I had never managed to get below 10 stone 9 pounds before the war. But when I came out of prison I was 9 stone 7 pounds. I can tell you, it soon went back on, though.'

There was not much he brought with him from IVB that he was likely to treasure. Only one object, in fact, and that he clung on to determinedly. It was a portrait, painted in oils on a canvas stuck on the back of a Red Cross supply box. The likeness is striking and even now, as it hangs on the wall in his study. 'It was done by a Russian, a skilled man, and I had to bribe my way into the Russian compound to have it painted. Three times I went in there, a couple of hours' sitting each time. It

36

was something to occupy us both, but I was pleased with the result.'

Geoffrey had seen six years' service in the RAF when he was demobbed. He returned home to find that Michael was already a capable horseman. The teaching had been carried out in his absence by a man named Harry Wigmore, constantly encouraged by Margaret. The riding bug had grabbed his son, and Geoffrey was certainly not disappointed.

'We rode together at point-to-point a few times. I remember on the first occasion that I was riding the favourite, but I spent so much time worrying about Michael and trying to look after him that I gave the race away!'

Now that he was back Geoffrey understandably felt no urge to travel. He just wanted to settle into normal life in the borders again. 'I spent four years in Canada before the war. There was not much work around in England during the thirties and it seemed the sensible thing to do. People talk about bad times in the 1980s, but no one who was around fifty years ago thinks anything of this recession.

'I believe every young man should travel a bit. It certainly did me no harm, and I found enough work out there to keep me going.

'It cost me £25 14s 2d to sail to Calgary and it took me three weeks to get there. I spent my twentieth birthday on Vancouver Island, and fifty years later I went back again on a holiday and spent my seventieth birthday in the same place. Only, the second time the journey took six hours. . . . Isn't it amazing, to think there could be that much difference during my lifetime?'

Geoffrey did not ride for long after the war. He turned to training, and produced a number of big-race winners from a relatively small yard. The family had moved into their current home, just west of Hereford, and gradually the demands of the farmland took over from the lure of the turf.

'It became increasingly difficult to do both. If I had plenty of horses in, it was always a toss-up whether the lads should ride out third lot in the afternoon or get on with the haymaking, and eventually the business side of it won.'

But if he withdrew from a financial involvement in racing, Geoffrey did not withdraw his interest. In succeeding years he had acted as starter for the local point-to-point, which he enjoyed, and judge, which he did not. He then graduated to the position of chairman, and there were few better-known figures in his own part of Herefordshire.

Very few people among the farms, smallholdings and hamlets of the border country are indifferent to racing, and the Scudamores, they feel, represent Herefordshire as much as they represent themselves.

At the 300-year-old house where the family's oldest living generation resided with their two small dogs, their garden and their memories, *The Sporting Life* was still delivered each day. 'One is not really enough,' mused Geoffrey. 'Margaret is Peter's greatest fan, you see, and she just about knocks me over each day in the rush to grab the *Life* first.'

Geoffrey died peacefully, following an illness. His funeral was attended, it seemed, by half the county. A Scudamore was gone, but he had lived long enough to see his grandson succeed, and yet another generation born.

4

'The Duke'

David Nicholson and his wife Dinah were standing on the stone steps outside Worcester's quaint, wooden changing rooms. The summer gloss was still apparent on the course as the field approached the final flight, directly in front of the couple. A young man with a driving style and a set expression of determination urged his mount over the obstacle and got down to ride his finish. Mrs Nicholson nudged her husband. 'There's your jockey,' she said. 'That's the boy you want.'

Being a greater exponent of the deadpan than the dramatic, David Nicholson did not exactly cry 'Eureka' and spring to get the jockey signed. 'I noted the missus' confidence,' he recalls, 'and I had seen enough for myself to realize she could be right. The boy had ability, that was obvious.'

As it transpired, the situation resolved itself admirably. Soon after that midweek race meeting in 1978, Peter Scudamore began regular riding-out for Nicholson at his Condicote stables. It was not long before the partnership graduated to more serious business and in a remarkably short period Dinah Nicholson's assertion was proved to be correct. Scudamore was indeed the man David wanted.

His choice of jockey was influenced, if only subconsciously, by his father, 'Frenchie'. A riding contemporary of legends like Fred Winter and Bob Turnell, Frenchie had later trained horses and jockeys in unique fashion, producing such as Michael Dickinson, Pat Eddery and Paul Cook. His traditionalist ideas had been implanted in his son David, who discovered a similar outlook in the Scudamores, father and son.

'It seemed quite natural that Peter should come here, and I was very pleased he did. His father Michael was a great friend to me when I was a jockey. He rode a lot for my father, and taught me a good deal about riding and, indeed, about life in general. We played cricket together regularly in the summers and often went to racing together in the winter. I was at his wedding and I was also at Wolverhampton the day that dreadful fall ended his career.

'Peter was a pageboy at our wedding and, as I knew the family so well, I watched him with interest when he started riding as an amateur. I remember particularly one day at Market Rasen. Peter was very impressive in a race won by my secretary of the time, Jo Champion, on Shermoon. So when Michael suggested that he might come to ride out here while working in Stow, I was delighted. I didn't know a great deal about his personality at the time, but I intended to find out.'

That sort of statement can sound formidable, coming from David Nicholson. Not for nothing is he called 'the Duke' by everyone in racing. His whole presence is imposing, his words carefully chosen and delivered with a quiet intent while his eyes weigh up the listener. He has the ability to make one feel nine years old again, quaking outside the headmaster's study, yet a moment later his face can break into a wreath of smiles, he can be offering drinks gaily and chatting about the fortunes of England's Test side. Cricket is his second love – it cannot compare with racing but it is something to get enthusiastic about during the summer – and stories abound of the Duke's temperamental exploits on a Sunday afternoon when the opposition, the umpire or even one of his own side had offended him. But in his own yard he is patently the guv'nor, no question. Respected by all of his twenty-eight lads, and probably held in a certain awe by some, he struts briskly between the boxes and barks the odd order. He is no ogre, though. Charm and humour come through, mixed, confusingly, with the touches of deliberate arrogance and aggression. He will make some

40

enemies, and no doubt has done, but one would bet that
he also makes close friends.

He began training in 1968, combining it with the
closing years of a riding career which brought him more
than 600 winners. 'Lots of people told me it couldn't be
done, and that I was a fool to carry on riding and train
at the same time. But, being the type I am, that just
made me more determined. I began with only seven
horses in my yard, and the following season I rode
seventy-one winners, my best ever figure.

'The good horses I had ridden over the years were
big, chasing types, including Mill House and Arkle, so
I set out optimistically to find a similar sort to train.
Lord Vestey was one of my first owners, and has several
in the yard still, and his preference was for 3-mile
chasers, which suited me admirably. I followed this
principle fairly successfully, buying big, backward and
unbroken horses from Ireland, despite the fact that my
father constantly told me I was mad. Everyone said I
could only train chasers and I was quite aware of the
criticism. But the horse which changed my pattern
arrived by accident.

'I was interested in a horse called Governor's Camp,
trained on the flat by John Dunlop down in Sussex.
When I phoned him he said that horse was not for sale,
but why didn't I go down to see something which was.
Knowing him as a genuine sort who would not waste
my time, I took him up on the offer, and the horse he
showed me was Broadsword. I bought him, found a
willing owner in Lord Northampton, and he has turned
out to be the best hurdler I have trained and one of the
best in the country.

'Around the same time some new owners came along
who wanted quicker returns than my usual style of horse
would offer. This is becoming the general trend – not
altogether surprising when you analyse the cost of being
an owner – but it did mean that I would benefit from a
change of emphasis. I began to buy more horses off the
flat, and the chasers I still bought from Ireland were
broken four-year-olds who would not wait too long for
a racecourse outing.

'Success brings success, of course, and when Broadsword's reputation spread, those in the yard gained in confidence and those outside sat up and took notice. We had forty-seven winners in the 1980–81 season and the knockers were now not knocking quite so hard. It was worth the change.'

The Duke can be intense when he talks about his horses, and he admits to an obsession for the sport. 'I enjoy all sports and will watch them avidly on television. But when it comes to racing I am a fanatic. I eat and sleep racing and talk of little else. I must be the most boring bloke in the world to live with. But I find that my life has accelerated over the years. There is not much time to stand around any more and I seem to be constantly gee'd up about the horses and their prospects. Maybe it is me, but probably it is the fact that we have become a successful yard. We have something to live up to.'

It did not escape public comment, nor Nicholson's attention, that the increased percentage of winers at his compact yard in little Condicote (population around 150) coincided approximately with the arrival at the yard of Mr P. Scudamore. The stable was on a low when 'Scu' arrived but partly through a clearing up of a virus among the horses and partly, no doubt, through the influx of fresh and ambitious new blood, the winners were soon ticking up again.

'I had plenty of jockeys available when Peter began riding-out here, but gradually things went wrong. Both Jeff King and Roy Mangan were injured, so the trickle of rides I had been able to give Peter early on increased quite dramatically.

'He won well on Jacko at Worcester, by which time I had formed a pretty firm opinion of him. There was no doubt that he was good material. The talent was there provided I could mould it, and steer him in the right direction. He was from a good background, intelligent and attentive and he had the ability to hold an interesting, articulate conversation whether it be about racing or something else. That set him apart from the pack for a start. And then there was his riding ability.

In a race he did what he was told, which is the first requisite so far as I am concerned. What is perhaps even more important, though, is that he had the ability to follow instructions and get himself in the right place – not every jockey has that. But he was not just a robot, he had flair too. Rough edges certainly, but for a young, inexperienced amateur he had plenty of promise.

'Maybe he was a bit too bouncy in his first year here. I don't discourage the lads from having something to say, but I don't want them getting above themselves. Peter might still have had something to learn in that department. I could see the signs because I had suffered from some of them myself – no good jockey should let emotion get the better of him, but we are all tempted sometimes. I shall never forget riding at Worcester years ago and being beaten by a neck on a horse of my father's. I knew I should have won and I was annoyed, but what I did was unforgivable. Instead of dropping my hands and quietly walking the horse back in the usual way, I whipped him round and galloped him back to the un-saddling enclosure. When I got off, still feeling angry with myself, my father hit me – not for losing the race but for behaving like a spoiled child. He was quite right too, and I never did it again.

'Peter upset me once at Cheltenham. It was one of the early meetings in the 1980–81 season, around October. He had been going quite well and no doubt his head was full of the idea that he should win every time he got on to the course. Well, he finished fourth on one of mine, and as he got off he said something stupid which plainly upset one of the horse's owners. I jumped on it straight away and sent him back to the weighing room, but it took me about three bottles of champagne to placate the owners. Later on I gave Scu the bollocking of his life. In a strange sense I believe that day did more for him than anything else.'

Only a month after that Cheltenham incident Nicholson was influential in the most important decision that Scudamore was to make. On Saturday, 17 November, while still an amateur and still acting as assistant trainer in the yard, Scudamore rode his ninth

winner of the season. Victory on Oakprime, for
Nicholson at Warwick, left him joint-leader in the
amateur jockeys' championship, but if he harboured
ambitions to win that title, he was never going to have'
the chance of living them out. The time had come to
join the professionals.

Conscience was pricking Scudamore by this stage.
While he had been working in the property business
there was never any question of turning pro as a jockey.
But for the past six months he had been devoting all his
energies to racing, and was being paid for his efforts in
the Condicote yard. As he says, 'Racing is a hard game
to get going in and riding as an amateur is the best way
of starting. But to me, anyone who works with horses
six or seven days a week cannot be regarded as a true
amateur. If I had gone on as I was, other jockeys and
people in the sport would have started to grumble, and
I would not have blamed them.'

So, only fifteen months after his maiden win on Rolyat,
and the dash to Devon in the old red banger, the
twenty-one-year-old made his decision at a Sunday
morning conference convened by Nicholson.

The trainer recalls, 'It is not a decision to be made
lightly. Once you have turned pro, there is no going
back, but Peter was clearly ready in terms of ability and
ambitious enough to make a go of it. I asked his parents
over, along with my father, and we discussed the situation together. No one was against the idea, not even
Peter's mother. I think she was well aware by that stage
that there was nothing whatever she could do to change
Peter's mind about riding, so if she couldn't beat him
she would join him.'

On the Monday morning the application form was
filled out and in the post to the Jockey Club. By
Wednesday Scudamore had lost his 'Mr' and was
cleared to ride at Worcester as a professional. He opened
his new career by picking up almost £200 in winning percentages as Sea Lane and Birshell gave him a memorable
double.

If anyone was more delighted for him than David

Nicholson it was Peter's father Michael. But, as he surveyed his son's spectacular start, he recalled, 'To think it took me seventy-six rides, and from August to March, before I rode my first winner as a professional . . . it took Peter about five minutes.'

5

Ups and Downs

Racing can be cruel, and I mean to its jockeys not its horses. Few other sports can give a competitor so much pleasure so quickly, only to snatch it back and inflict an equal dose of pain. Peter Scudamore sampled a generous share of both during his first few months as a professional jockey and emerged a more philosophical man than when he set out.

In the space of only ten weeks he rode a remarkable twenty-four winners and from being a promising amateur with a familiar name he had suddenly leap-frogged into the leading group of professionals. But the first race of a midweek card at Haydock Park on 6 February cut short his euphoria in the most freakish manner imaginable.

Peter's success had attracted the admiring attention of several outside trainers, large and small. They did not come much larger than Fred Rimell, however, and after parting company with his stable jockey, Colin Tinkler, he decided on Scudamore as the ideal replacement. Going through the courteous channels of diplomacy, Rimell contacted David Nicholson and asked if he would release his jockey to ride for him whenever possible. Nicholson agreed on the understanding that all bookings for Scudamore were passed through him, and suddenly the rookie professional was riding for not one, but two of the country's most prominent trainers.

His first ride for Rimell was a winner – Swashbuckling in a novice hurdle at Ascot on 11 January – and such was the strength of the ammunition now at his disposal that Scudamore had risen to eighth place in the jockeys' championship, a distance behind the runaway leader Jonjo O'Neill, when fate decreed that he had tasted enough of the sweet life for the time being.

The sixth of February was a filthy day. Rain slanted down from a slate-grey sky and those hardy souls who had braved the conditions for the punting and socializing huddled beneath the stands at the well-appointed Lancashire course just off the M6 motorway. The day contained three booked rides from Rimell for Scudamore, the most promising of which was undoubtedly the five-year-old hurdler Brian's Venture in the opening race.

It was the horse's third run of the season. He had been unplaced at Kempton and then, as a well-backed favourite when ridden by Jeff King at Nottingham, blew up on the run-in and finished third, having looked a certain winner. The Haydock contest was competitive, with twenty-two runners, but Brian's Venture started second favourite and Scudamore was optimistic.

The race did not go to plan. Holding up his mount for a late challenge, Scudamore produced him at the second last but found no further gears. Brian's Venture finished fourth and Scudamore was pulling him up, feeling a shade dejected, when there was a shout behind him and, before he had time to react, a shooting pain assaulted his right leg and he slumped forward over the horse's neck.

His leg was broken in two places below the knee, the result of an almost unbelievable collision. Sam Morshead, a close friend of Scudamore's, had yelled a warning too late for Peter to avoid an out-of-control tailender, which cannoned into Brian's Venture, trapping and snapping Peter's leg between the two horses.

Few people around, either jockeys or spectators, were aware of what had happened. Up in the stand even Mary Scudamore had missed it. Having watched the race with her normal nervous, compulsive reluctance, she had hurried away to be at the unsaddling enclosure when the horses returned. She remembers vividly the sight of Peter slowly coming through the rain and the drenched groups of watchers, still bent forward and now quite obviously suffering. 'I just could not understand what had happened,' she says. 'He had looked perfectly all right at the end of the race and I had felt relieved, as usual. But now I was in a panic.'

Scudamore was taken to the local hospital where the leg was set and put in plaster. His parents, meanwhile, stayed to watch their own stable achieve a rare winner with Sointulla Boy; somehow the excitement they should have felt was not there.

By the following morning Peter was sitting in a soft armchair in the front room of his parents' Hoarwithy home. His plastered leg was propped on a pile of cushions, a collection of well-thumbed Dick Francis thrillers lay beside him. But he had read all the books before, and already he was bored.

Moody flicking through the racing papers only depressed him more as he surveyed forthcoming races and horses he would have ridden if only. . . . His one consolation was the continuing foul weather and the fact that two meetings had already been abandoned.

He was not bitter about the accident. No one was to blame, he said, and anyway, he had been having a good run. Something had to go wrong some time. His father, looking on benignly from across the room, winked and added, 'I would never tell his mother but I knew, as we all did, that Peter was going to get hurt at times. It is part of the job and he is man enough to take it and fight back.'

'Up to a fortnight before,' muses Peter, 'I had hardly had a fall in two months – not since I turned professional, in fact. I was cocky about it all, imagining I was good enough not to need any luck. But then I had four falls in two weeks, and then that. I will have to accept injuries for as long as I ride, but that doesn't make it any easier at the time.

'The oddest thing was the plague of injuries affecting people around me. Allen Webb, who shared a cottage with me, had broken his neck. And Roy Mangan, who lived just down the road, had broken his kneecap. It seemed it was my turn.'

Although he kept his sanity by kidding himself he might recover in time for a first ride in the Grand National, there was really no hope. It was the end of Peter's season, a season in which he had established himself more dramatically than ever he realized at the time.

'Only when I look back now, three seasons on, can I appreciate just how fast things happened that year. From the time I left the estate agents' job I seldom seemed to be off a horse's back. I had spent the summer in Ireland, going round the country with one of their jockeys, John Harty, and working for Jim Bolger, who also gave me a few rides. He put me up on a horse called Pigeon's Nest in the big amateur handicap during a flat meeting at Galway, and it was my only important winner on the level. I met a lot of kind people that summer and came back a good bit wiser about racing.

'Once I had turned professional everything fell into place, almost too neatly to be true. It was flattering for a newcomer like myself to attract rides from a trainer as famous as Fred Rimell, and there was a stage when his offer to go there full time as stable jockey the following year seemed extremely tempting. But while I was laid up with my broken leg I pondered on the decision and opted to stay with David. Loyalty was one good reason, but not the only one. While David had been very good to me, he had also been building up a very promising yard of horses, and I felt we would do well the next season.

'My first priority, however, was to get fit. I chose to spend the summer on a working break in Scandinavia. My father had introduced me to a number of his friends and acquaintances in both Norway and Sweden during our holidays there years earlier, and I managed to fix myself up with some daily work and some race-riding.

'Norway and Sweden only have one or two jump races each week, but I was able to ride in some flat races too, which improved my style in riding a finish.

'I based myself in Oslo and rode work on the track there most mornings. We started very early, something like five o'clock usually, but by nine it was finished and the rest of the day was mine to enjoy. At least by getting up early and working I felt I was doing something positive to keep in trim. I have been back twice since, and

49

it always gives me a decent break. I come home feeling fit and aware, with a fresh mind and a lot of enthusiasm. I can wind down while keeping in touch with racing, and the contacts I have made will hopefully provide further openings for me to ride in Europe on Sundays, something I would like to do far more regularly than I do now.'

The Englishman abroad can occasionally be an arrogant animal, however, and Scudamore admits to having transgressed in this respect on one occasion in Sweden.

'I went there feeling superior, believing that because I was an English jockey I must be better than this bunch of Swedish amateurs. And during the race there I behaved in similar fashion, going up the inside in a cheeky way I would not have attempted at home. After that several of the Swedes cut up rough during the race, and afterwards I had a series of rows in the weighing room. But although I might have argued my case at the time, I know I was wrong. I had approached them with entirely the wrong attitude and I was asking for trouble. They got nasty with me because I deserved it. It taught me a lesson and I always treated foreign jockeys with respect after that. In return, they have been very friendly towards me.

'The lifestyle in Oslo was very appealing. I made some good friends, whom I still stay with each time I go over, and I found I was able to do things which I had almost forgotten I enjoyed. Simple things, like spending an evening at a disco or nightclub and having a few drinks, are just not on during an English season, especially for me because I never have been able to drink a lot and still be at my best the next day. I know a number of jockeys who can, and there are times when I envy them, but in my case the only social occasions I commit myself to, when I am riding the following day, are the very occasional dinners.

'So the Oslo nightclubs, lively and friendly places, made a refreshing change for me, and I was able to go in the certain knowledge that no one would know who I was. In England, I am sometimes recognized at parties and although I am very happy to have an intelligent conversation on racing and horses any time of the day or night, enjoyment of an evening can be spoiled by a drunken bore asking stupid questions. I don't enjoy idle talk, which is probably a fault, but I am also suspicious that people may inflate my drinking from a half of beer to being drunk if I get beaten the next day.'

Scudamore came home to Condicote a day or so before the start of the 1980–81 season, and reported himself fully fit. The bookmakers took little notice and installed Jonjo O'Neill as firm favourite to retain his jockeys' title. John Francome was next in the betting at 3–1 and no one else featured. Anyone fancying Peter's prospects could have received very favourable odds for a wager – but then, in all honesty, he probably did not even fancy himself.

'I had no realistic hope whatsoever of being champion. Jonjo and John were still somewhere in the clouds as far as I was concerned, and if someone had told me I would ride even as many as fifty winners, I would have been staggered. But by halfway through the season fifty seemed nothing, and it gradually dawned on me that I had a real chance of being champion. Jonjo had broken his leg very badly at Bangor in October and by soon after Christmas the championship had resolved itself into a race between John and myself. I was always a few behind, but even through the major meetings of March I did not lose touch, and by the time April arrived I felt I could catch him. I had plenty of promising rides left, probably more than John in fact, and my trainers were helping out as much as possible by keeping their horses going.

'In racing terms, I was living from day to day. Probably I was a little bemused about it, but because it was so unexpected I felt no pressure at all.'

Francome, the supremely artistic horseman from Swindon, who is attached to Fred Winter's Lambourn yard, had jumped to the understandable conclusion that, barring a mishap, his main danger had passed with the early exit of champion O'Neill. Now he was being seriously extended, and he jokes, 'I kept telling Scu that he ought to go on holiday for a week or two. I remember seeing him for the first time in an amateur riders' hurdle race at Fakenham a couple of years earlier, and being convinced at the time that I had spotted a future champion. He rode a superb finish and I would have had to be blind not to be impressed. I asked Oliver Sherwood, our assistant trainer, who the hell the rider was. I honestly didn't have a clue, but I know him only too well now. He kept going tremendously well that year. He was dedicated and very serious – too serious in my view because he hardly ever smiled. He probably made the mistake of thinking he should win on everything, and then being upset when he didn't.'

But Francome, whose constant humour and frivolity conceal a powerful motivation, was to be released from his pursuer on the first evening of May.

Scudamore's total had risen to ninety-one winners and he trailed Francome by only five, with five weeks of the season remaining. Before racing at Taunton that night I had recorded interviews with them both for a sports programme's feature on the championship the following day. By the end of the evening I could have thrown the tapes away because the title race was over.

This time Scudamore's fate was a more orthodox fall. After two broken bones received without even losing his seat on the horse, he came to grief in horrifying fashion along the back straight at Taunton.

'I was riding one of our own horses called Salad. He was owned by Ben Brooks, a man who supports both David and myself very loyally, but Salad could be a temperamental sort and never quite suited my style. We were approaching the first fence down the back when the horse chickened out and slid into it on his back legs. I fell, though not too heavily, and was thinking I had survived a nasty moment when I was kicked on the back of the head by another passing horse.

'Although I never lost consciousness I knew at once that it could be bad. Instinctively, I did not move, just lay there until I felt something odd, put by hand up to my ear and brought it away covered in blood. I was not in pain, but now I was really frightened.

52

'The ambulance collected me and took me to the local hospital, where I stayed for a few days. They told me I had a hairline fracture of the skull and they had to keep waking me every hour of the day and night. They did not tell me why, but I understand it was in case I lapsed into a coma, another prospect I found rather scary.

'I forced myself to look on the bright side. It would have been all too easy to lie there feeling sorry for myself, but I was actually fortunate to have escaped so lightly. When I inspected my helmet later the paint had been chipped away and a mark left by the horse's shoe.

'I reflected how my father used to ride with a flimsy cork helmet which would have offered precious little protection against such a kick. And David Nicholson tells me he rode with no helmet at all on the flat. I had often been critical of the modern helmet and even now I think the harness stretches and moves too much for it to be truly effective. A motorbike helmet might look stupid on a racecourse but it would be the only secure insurance. But still, my helmet had done its job. The kick had fractured my skull, but without a helmet there is no doubt I would have been dead.'

Michael and Mary Scudamore were not present at Taunton that night. A phone call informed them of Peter's injury and after a fretful night they drove down to Taunton the following morning to visit him in hospital. Michael admits, 'We were both worried. It sounded a bad one, and any head injury is a cause for concern. But our fears were eased when we walked into the ward and saw him. He was sitting up in bed, his head swathed in bandages, but looking remarkably cheerful, with Marilyn his wife on one side and Lorna Vincent the leading girl jockey on the other. I knew he was okay then!'

The potential seriousness of the injury, and Peter's natural concern for his own wellbeing, were such that a full twenty-four hours passed before the consequence of his position hit him. 'I looked at the racing results on the Saturday night and saw that I had missed two winners at Worcester. Only then did it occur to me that I had conceded the championship by default. For a few hours afterwards I was terribly depressed about it.

'Within three weeks I was riding again. I knew there was no chance of catching John now, for although he had hardly been setting the world alight in my absence he was a dozen or more ahead of me and only a few racing days remained. Knowing that, people told me I was stupid to come back so quickly and tried to persuade me to rest up for the following season. But I knew in my own mind that I was doing the right thing. I had visited a specialist in Cheltenham and my head wound had been cleared. I was suffering no headaches, no after-effects at all in fact, and even on my first ride back I did not consciously worry about my head. If I had, it would have been a sign that my nerve was wavering, and that would have been dangerous.

'Whether or not it was sensible, the decision was made utterly worthwhile when I won on Rapallo for father at one of the end-of-season Stratford meetings. He had not enjoyed the best of seasons, and it was a thrill for me to be able to help cheer him up. Other than that I must admit I hardly had a decent ride, and I clocked off for the season with ninety-one winners, still clear in second place and still wondering what might have happened but for that fall at Taunton.

'But I could not allow myself to dwell on the past. There wasn't time, anyway. The day after the season ended I flew to Stockholm to ride in their two major jumping events of the year, and quite by coincidence I gave myself the sternest of fitness tests.

'Swedish racing is not strong, but I rode the favourite in their champion hurdle. He slipped up on a bend and deposited me on the floor. I survived that one without any damage and went on to ride another fancied horse in the Swedish National. All was going well, and I was quietly confident of our chances, when a horse in front of me, ridden by a Frenchman, fell heavily. There was no room to take avoiding action and my horse hit the fallen animal squarely up the backside, giving me a crude ejector-seat treatment.

'I came down on my head and got up feeling perfectly all right. A little bruised in body and spirit maybe, but with no lasting damage and no mental hurdles to climb.

Perhaps, I thought to myself as for the second time I trudged back to the weighing room without a horse, it was all meant. At least I knew beyond doubt then that the Taunton fall would not come back to haunt me.'

Scudamore returned to Condicote in the final week of July 1981. There was little for him to do in the Nicholson yard until the new season was under way; the stable lads were kept employed, walking the horses on the roads – work which can leave the keenest horseman both bored and saddlesore – but the stable jockey was not called upon before the time came to school the yard's string, sharpening them up for the campaign ahead.

This time the bookies were taking no chances. With O'Neill likely to be out until Christmas, still suffering from his broken leg, Francome and Scudamore were bracketed almost together in the betting. And that was how they would stay.

6

The Condicote Method

Soccer seasons start with a fanfare of television specials, newspaper countdowns and players' puerile quotes. Each cricket season begins with a showcase match at Lord's. The flat-racing season attracts a mass of media coverage for its traditional launch at Doncaster in March. But National Hunt racing resumes in the final week of July each year, limping apologetically on to the sporting calendars like an unwanted stranger using the back entrance.

It has always been the same and I doubt if it will ever change. In many ways the English climate is to blame; racecourse surfaces are invariably so boneshakingly hard for jumping during August and September that no trainer is going to risk too many of his better horses breaking down before the season is properly under way. Consequently, the racing which does take place generally consists either of small fields or poor horses or both, and for two months at least some unfamiliar names, both equine and human, will appear among the winners.

For top jockeys, even finding horses to ride can be taxing work until the major stables begin to produce their goods, and a liaison with one of the crop of trainers based in the West Country is virtually essential to anyone seeking a decent start. Traditionally much of the early racing takes place at two courses no more than ten miles apart – Devon and Exeter, high on Haldon Hill overlooking the city, and Newton Abbot, farther down the holiday road towards Torquay. The reason is straightforward economic sense: holidaymakers are gathered in the area as a captive audience, and money through the turnstiles is gold dust to tracks which live permanently on a knife-edge through the precarious winter weather, which may devour any number of scheduled fixtures.

But, while the West Country courses are reaping some profit, and the bookmakers are taking their share from the habitual punters who care not whether they bet on a supposed good thing at Devon or Cheltenham, most jockeys are driving an enormous number of miles for a single ride, or maybe two, and many will scarcely be in the black for the season come the end of September.

Peter Scudamore could scarcely claim a poverty-stricken start, but he still did not consider the 1981–82 season had properly begun until 26 September. 'That was the day of the first televised jumps meeting, at Stratford, and also the day on which David Nicholson brought out a couple of his better horses for their pipe-openers. Conna Valley, who was running over fences for the first time, finished third and was most encouraging, and then Lucky Call, one of our really consistent chasers, was second. The following Saturday, at Chepstow, Conna Valley ran again and won. It was David's first success of the season and the signal that everything was really under way.

'It would be wrong of me to complain about the early weeks of the season, or certainly about the earliest days. I had been booked by Neville Callaghan, who trains mainly flat-race horses in Newmarket, to partner Can-do-More on the opening day at Market Rasen. The horse was well known anyway, having been placed the previous season and run well on the flat, and it was clearly a good catch for me right at the start. He duly won, and two days later I was on the two-winner mark when Prairie Master came in at Newton Abbot. I was delighted with the horse then, not so pleased with him nine months later when he put me back in hospital. . . .

'Following that fast getaway, though, I really slowed down. The next few weeks were difficult because I had no attachments down in the west, whereas John Francome was picking up regular rides from Les Kennard and John Thorne.

'John does not spend many nights away during a season but he often stays down in Devon during the opening weeks. He likes to play some tennis, and as most of his rides are on the local courses it makes sense. My position is slightly different. I have to look elsewhere for some rides, and in any case the Duke likes me to be available for riding out in the mornings. Sometimes that can be a bind, but I look upon it as being beneficial in two ways – it is a discipline, which is important in my lifestyle, and it frequently helps me to learn something new about individual horses and how best they should be ridden.'

In Michael Scudamore's time as a jockey many riders did as Francome does now, and booked into hotels or guest houses for two or three weeks by the Devon coast. 'It was like an extension of the summer break with a few rides thrown in,' he recalls. 'With a lot of jockeys together, the evenings were frequently pretty lively, especially when there was no racing next day. It was a pleasant, leisurely way to start the season, and staying down made practical sense, too, before the motorways cut hours off the journey.'

Peter reflects, 'Most jockeys, I think, prefer to ride good horses on softer ground than you can find in August or September. But for some, they are very good months. I remember Jeff King riding nine winners before the end of September one year – all on the same horse, Roman Holiday. Something similar happened last year with a horse called Silversmith, who loves the hard ground and enjoys plenty of racing. He had won five times, mostly ridden by Steve Smith Eccles, before many of the good horses had appeared on a course at all.

'The West Country meetings can be good fun. The weather is usually good, and the crowd is generally in a holiday mood. The biggest crowds come to these meetings when the weather is dull but dry. On sunny days they go on the beach and on wet days they sit in their hotels, it seems.'

Apart from the occasional game of cricket, Scudamore does not play any other sports, so he has a pre-season training routine to shake off any summer excesses. It is nothing like as vigorous as a footballer's training, for instance, but then the demands are very different.

'A jockey can only get race-fit by race-riding, because muscles are used which never come into play in any other sports or exercises. But to sharpen myself up I do some running and cycling during each July. If I am in Oslo, I will run the mile to the nearest swimming pool, then have a swim and run back again. When I am back in England, and perhaps not riding for very many races, I put on my tracksuit and cycle a few miles – that is quite far enough around the Cotswold hills!'

Far more complicated than the jockey's fitness, however, is that of the horse. In Condicote this is exclusively David Nicholson's province, and he admits he derives more satisfaction from the early weeks of any season as a trainer than ever he did as a jockey. 'When the horses come back into the yard in July they resume their daily work on the gallops and the roads. But it is mid-August before I start any schooling – just a few at a time, given a pop over some hurdles, rather like a cricketer having a net at the end of March. Most of them know the game already; this is just to remind them they can do it. The most exciting time for me is October. I have a pretty good idea which of my horses are going to perform well, but there is always the odd surprise, good or bad, and the first full schooling sessions give the biggest clues. All of them will have had their preliminary schools by this time, so I organize sessions on three successive Thursday mornings. Peter and Steve Smith Eccles, my two retained jockeys, will both come down, and between them they will school the lot each week. Sometimes I have gone back to the house after one of those sessions feeling absolutely elated. But that doesn't always happen, of course.

'Once those three sessions are finished I will only do the occasional piece of schooling – perhaps a horse who has lost his confidence after a fall, or one who is graduating from hurdles to fences. But there must be a reason for doing it. Jumping, I always think, is a mental thing for a horse and they will always do it better if they can enjoy it, as I try to make it fun for them when they are schooled here.

'The three-year-olds, about to go hurdling for the first time, are an individual case. I will often school them the day after they arrive in the yard. That way, they get it into their heads that it must be good for them, and the grounding they receive from that initial session can last them the rest of their racing lives.'

Scudamore is as enthusiastic as his boss over the early-morning schooling sessions. He is habitually at the yard by seven in the morning, anyway, for routine riding-out work, but the schooling is more fulfilling.

'Sometimes we can school forty horses in a session, between Steve and myself,' he says. 'It is a good way of doing it, even if it takes a long time – up to three hours in two lots.

'The exciting part is that you know these are the horses who will effectively guide your season. I am always conscious that if they take to jumping, whether it be hurdles or fences, I have a far better chance of piling up some winners as the season progresses. So it is more than just a job of work to me – it is an investment in my own future.'

Nicholson's stable lads ride their own horses out on to the schooling grounds and sit on them until it is their turn to be schooled. Scudamore and Smith Eccles, meanwhile, are schooling one, discussing its performance with Nicholson, then jumping on another and beginning the process again.

'David has excellent facilities. Everyone in racing knows that he is outstanding at teaching a horse his job before he ever sees a racecourse. A typical programme for a three-year-old about to start his hurdling career would be to begin with a few jumps over baby logs, then progress to sleepers and baby hurdles, finally giving him a jump over a portable racing fence, about the size of a hurdle but with a soft top which teaches the horse to brush through and quicken up his jumping.

'Once the guv'nor is satisfied that he has completed that course all right, the horse will have a run, followed by one or two further schools and a second run. He may not be schooled again after that. People wonder why a horse who has run decently first time out should have to go back for another school, but the fact is they are often frightened by being in a race for the first time, especially if there are a lot of runners, some of which will be blundering into and through the hurdles. The intermediate school is simply to restore any lost confidence.

'Novice chasers have a similar programme, but as they are older and know a bit about racing, the extent of their schooling depends very much on the horse. The aims are to produce horses who are brave, but sensible.

'Very few of our horses turn out to be cowards because we progress with them, giving them a chance at every stage of the jumping ladder. If they don't get confidence from the way David brings them on, they are no good for this game.

'Some are strange cases. We have had a horse in the yard some time now who can't jump a hurdle and certainly wouldn't jump a fence. But we know, from going back through his family, that he is quite likely to take to it when he is seven or eight years old. It is annoying at the time, but it is another thing which teaches patience.

'Another of our horses fell first time out over fences, came back and had another school, then went and won his next race. We thought he must have his confidence back, but when he fell again, in his first race the following season, he just decided he had seen enough and made it very plain he did not want to jump anything ever again. That is naturally disappointing but occasionally bound to happen.

'The most difficult and hazardous part of a jockey's job comes when he is aboard an obviously scared animal. I can only liken it to Niki Lauda setting off in the Monaco Grand Prix knowing that his car had defective steering or brakes – he wouldn't do it, but now and again a jockey has to get on a horse and try to put back the defective parts.

'Basically, a jockey needs to be certain that when he approaches an obstacle and tells the horse to jump the order will be obeyed. The alternative is an unpleasant

fall and no jockey likes to start a race knowing that the
existing chance of coming off has already been multi-
plied. The Duke knows that I will not ride a horse
properly unless I have confidence in him, because my
life really is in the horse's hands.

'The pleasure comes, however, when I ride a horse
first time out who meets every obstacle perfectly and
comes back wanting more. I go back into the weighing
room and feel I want to talk someone through it, jump
by jump. Hywell Davies thinks the same way, and
usually he and I tell each other how wonderful our
horses were and go through the race in great detail. It
is exciting to me, and I feel someone who does not get
pleasure from that experience is probably not a real
jockey.'

Scudamore, unlike many jockeys, has no preference
between chasers and hurdlers. 'Class is all that matters.
A bad horse will always be flat out between the obstacles,
which means if he does not meet it right, the rider has
no chance. The good horses meet the jumps with time
to spare; you know how good they are simply by the feel
they give you. It might be stating the obvious, but in
this game a horse will win nothing unless he jumps well.'

So it is back to the schooling grounds at Condicote,
and David Nicholson, who rides very little these days
but knows the jumping game as well as anyone, gives
his orders. Peter explains, 'David tells Steve and me
which horses to ride and when. He says what each horse
should jump and, to a degree, how fast we should go.
After each horse has done his school, we both say what
we think. Sometimes I give the opinion that one is all
right and jumps well enough, but I sense he is not
satisfied. But generally we think very similarly about
horses. It is the same as racing – our immediate thoughts
after a race very often coincide, and David frequently
knows exactly what I will say before I have even come
in to unsaddle.'

Early-season business at Condicote is not confined to
the schooling grounds, but Nicholson and his jockey
enter into it all with a dedication which indicates just
why they have become such a formidable partnership in

recent seasons. The trainer explains the importance of these initial months:

'It is at this early stage of the season that all the work is done so far as the horses are concerned. They have had their summer away and, naturally enough, they come back unfit. So we have them out for an hour and threequarters each day, six days a week, to get them physically hard – and they will canter four times a week to clear their pipes. When we are in full swing I have the resources to get thirty horses out first lot, and I need to, with more than fifty in the yard.

'Everyone is keen to get the horses running, not least Peter and myself. But there is no benefit from rushing horses in on surfaces like concrete which they are just going to hate. They can sour a horse for some time even if he comes back sound – a lot break down and can be out for the season. So I will run nothing until the ground is suitable, and my better horses will generally not be seen out before October at the earliest.'

In the intervening weeks, however, Cotswold House is campaign headquarters and the planning gathers pace, while out in the yard head lad Lyn Burrows, starting his fourth season with Nicholson, organizes his own troops, cracking the whip now and again but generally encouraging the spirit of humour and camaraderie which any good yard brings out in its lads.

One major event takes place at the yard in mid-August, before a single one of the stable inmates has been seen on a racecourse. This is Nicholson's Open Day, when members of the public are invited for a conducted tour of the stables and a preliminary peek at the horses in training for the new season.

'It began in a very small way,' says Nicholson. 'We thought it was a good idea and a couple of hundred people showed up. I took them round and chatted to them about the horses, and we had a barbecue afterwards. All very civilized, but quite low key. We planned it again in 1981, for the middle Sunday in August, and this time it attracted a bit more publicity. I had an ox-roast organized and the lads were all here to help. But in the middle of the morning I was still indoors when one of them came to me and said there was a long queue outside. He was right – 1700 people came that day and the place was overrun. Luckily, I was able to get a Tannoy system at short notice and we muddled through with a spot of improvisation. But it does seem to be a popular event and for 1982 we got the rest of the village more involved.'

Nicholson was astonished by the enthusiasm of his visitors, some of whom had travelled from as far afield as North Yorkshire and Devon just for the day. But his stentorian commentary, interspersing the odd wisecrack with a wise tip or two, did much to make their journeys worthwhile, and the whole occasion smacked pleasantly of the village carnivals of long ago.

No one, including Nicholson and Scudamore, is in much doubt about the star of the yard and, even in August of 1981, the word on most people's lips was Broadsword. Narrowly and unexpectedly beaten into second place in the juvenile hurdler's championship, the *Daily Express* Triumph Hurdle, at Cheltenham in March, he was now being aimed at the Champion Hurdle, taking in most of the major events open to him along the way.

By his efforts of the previous season he had won a special place in the affections of his trainer and jockey and, like so many outstanding performers on the track, he had plenty of character to couple with his ability. He is even given a box to suit his personality. Very often a handsome head will now peer round to survey you from a corner wooden box in the top yard. From this privileged position Broadsword can look out on most of his colleagues and snatch a sneak preview of whoever is approaching from the lower yard. His ears are pricked and his eyes sparkle, a vivid advert for the theory that racehorses relish every minute of their lives.

Scudamore's first liaison of the season with Broadsword was on 22 October at Newbury. He started favourite but was beaten into second place by Ra Tapu, a horse trained in Epsom with only moderate form to recommend it. Nicholson denied that he was disappointed at the time and promised that his horse would improve dramatically for having a race behind him,

e stable girl looks more animated than the jockey, but this was Peter Scudamore's
t winner as a professional, on Gambling Prince at Worcester, November 1979

Right: One of Peter's earliest rides

Below: As a pageboy at David Nicholson's wedding, with the legendary 'Frenchie' Nicholson on the far right

PETER·SCUDAMORE, first

...cepting the Amoco Jockey of the Month Award, March 1982. The picture in the ...ckground shows Peter's previous win in December, about which he remembers little, ...ng concussed at the time

...ur generations of Scudamores. Grandfather Geoffrey, who died in December 1982, ...ter with his wife Marilyn and son Thomas, and father Michael

Peter rides a driving finish on Bustello in a steeplechase at Aarau, Switzerland, during May 1981

This mistake cost Peter the race, but he and Fury Boy remained intact

which in time he did. But as Scudamore says, 'I thought we were only kidding ourselves about that race. He was not at his peak, that's true enough, but at the time I misguidedly felt he should have won that race if he was a true champion hurdler.'

So already, with the season still in its infancy, Scudamore was thinking ahead to the major events of March and April. More immediately, he had the biggest pre-Christmas chase, the Hennessy Gold Cup, as an objective, and this deliberate forward planning was an early sign of the new pressures upon him.

'In the past I had looked no further ahead than the next day, or possibly the next weekend for the big Saturday meeting. I was not in a position to regulate my rides weeks in advance because I had not achieved anything to warrant the trainers' cooperation. But now I was in a new situation. Things were expected of me and I had to be more aware of forthcoming races. It was an added pressure, but one which I enjoyed. In September and October, for instance, each time I rode a decent 3-mile handicap chaser I would get off after the race trying to assess in my own mind whether it was of sufficient quality for the Hennessy or the Mackeson. If it was, I might mention my thoughts to the trainer and hope he might have it entered and offer me the ride. If, however, I decided that the horse was just not good enough, I would try to persuade the trainer not to run it in the big events, to save the embarrassment of possibly having to turn down a ride, which comes hard to any jockey.'

Scudamore's choice for the Hennessy was made straightforward when he won on Captain John at Ascot for Greek owner Michael Mouskos, one of racing's eccentrics. Mouskos makes a habit of changing trainers and jockeys several times a season and has repeatedly been refused a licence to train his string himself – a story which resulted in some colourful quotes later in the season as Mouskos gave his personal opinion of the Jockey Club.

But, at this stage of the season, Scudamore was the man in favour with Mouskos, and following his impressive win at Ascot he was booked for the Hennessy at

Newbury in November. In the week before the big race Scudamore drove to Newmarket to ride Captain John in a workout – a privilege for which jockeys are paid no extra; it is seen as part of their race plan and they will phlegmatically consider it an extra opportunity to familiarize themselves with the horses' habits. In this case, Scudamore came away feeling confident, with one looming reservation.

'Captain John was given 11 stone 2 pounds to carry, which I thought was too much. Josh Gifford's Approaching had been backed to beat us in the Ascot race at level weights. When he fell at the second fence it actually told the handicapper nothing, yet in the Hennessy he was rated 8 pounds better off, which left me very puzzled. The handicapper appeared to have assessed Captain John on what he was capable of rather than what he had achieved, and the difference was substantial. But having said all that, I would still have chosen my horse if everything in the field had been offered to me.'

Neither Approaching nor Captain John won the Hennessy. The brandy prize went to Fulke Walwyn, who had won it four times before in his marathon training career and had recently celebrated his seventy-first birthday. No one begrudged this grand old man another slice of success, but Michael Mouskos went away believing that Captain John was still the best chaser in England, and Peter Scudamore went away to plan for the following week – and the one after that.

7

Treble Chance

Sunday morning at Cotswold House. For many, the time is not advanced enough for anything more exacting than propping pillows against the bedhead, spreading the newspapers across the duvet and reaching blearily for the coffee. But inside Condicote's best-known property the lads have been on the move around the yard for hours, and now the office is open and the weekly management conference is under way.

Racing stables exist, in the final analysis, on winners. A yard will never be full for long if the success rate dries up, as current owners will become disenchanted and potential owners will look elsewhere. But even with a yard of good horses, winners are not guaranteed, and much of the success is orchestrated by shrewd placement of the right horse in the right race, taking into account the course, the conditions of the race, conditions underfoot and the strength of the opposition. Of these prerequisites, only the first two are known when provisional entries have to be lodged three weeks in advance of each race. So further contemplation is necessary at much shorter notice, and this is what occupies Messrs Nicholson and Scudamore each Sunday.

The office is one of the newest innovations at the Nicholson base and, although constructed in basic style, contains everything necessary for its purpose. A television stands in one corner, with a video unit parked underneath and a row of cassettes alongside. Nicholson is supplied, as a matter of course, with video tapes of his horses whenever they run in a televised race; he also records other races himself, and pores over them at great length to assess the merits of his own horses and other people's. Scudamore also has a video at home and studies his own rides time after time to see what went right, or what went wrong.

A desk unit runs round three walls of the compact office, with an open diary, a filing system and an entry book. The shelves above contain books about racing and further files, while hanging on the wall is a photograph of more than thirty male guests at David's wedding in 1962. Every one of them had ridden winners under rules.

In this room, built just outside the back door of the mainhouse, David and Peter work their way through the forthcoming week's race meetings, deciding which of their entries should run and who should ride what.

Nicholson explains: 'I try to look as far as ten days ahead, chiefly to give Peter and Steve a good idea of where they will be required to ride. I feel it is very important that the trainer does not mess his jockeys around any more than is necessary in the natural course of the job. I have a Prestel system on my television, through which I can see the four-day acceptors for meetings the day before they appear in *The Sporting Life*. This gives us a clearer impression of the week ahead when we talk on Sunday and we can be pretty definite about what is going to run, at least up to Thursday.

'Scu has generally been approached by outside trainers asking him to ride for them, but he will not confirm anything until we have made our internal decisions. Sometimes he is very enthusiastic about riding a particular horse for someone else, and if that is the case I will do my best to help make certain he is available. But that does not mean I will compromise my own stable to suit someone else's and occasionally I have to be firm.'

Nicholson finds the planning can be among the most exhilarating parts of his job. 'It is sometimes too easy to get an inflated opinion of your own horses and imagine they can beat anything, but nevertheless I love sitting down and mapping out their programmes. It gives me a thrill to feel that they are in races they should win.

The anticipation is sometimes more fulfilling than the reality, of course, but thankfully not always.'

Scudamore is as engrossed in the routine as his boss because he is equally dedicated to the business of finding winners. In his case, however, the operation is more delicate. He has to settle his commitments to his own yard and then satisfy the wishes of other interested trainers, while convincing himself that he is accepting suitable rides. In 1981–82 he rode for his father, whenever he was available, and also formed an arrangement with David Morley from Bury St Edmunds, who had a small yet select string of jumpers and had just split with his long-serving jockey, Bob Davies.

Nicholson and Morley, in particular, were responsible for a large percentage of his rides, and reached an immediate understanding that the former's first claim would never be jeopardized. This caused no problems for Scudamore; his headaches arose mainly from the smaller trainers, naturally anxious to secure the services of a successful jockey for their horses but occasionally lacking understanding when he was unavailable.

'There is no doubt that the little trainers, with only a few horses in their yard, put me under pressure at times. It is a satisfying pressure because it means I am in demand, and no jockey should ever complain about that, but it is nevertheless a vicious circle. If you don't ride winners, the small trainers will not be very interested in you. If you do ride plenty of winners, they will mostly be supplied by one or two strong trainers; the outside rides are a bonus, often one-off affairs and seldom to be considered as a permanent ride. But certain trainers have been put out when I have turned down one of their horses to ride something else. Clearly I don't want to upset them because every trainer is a potential employer, but in being diplomatic about it I also have to be firm. If I decide that one horse has a better winning chance than another, and I am offered both rides, I will take the likelier winner. Just as placing horses correctly is one of the skills of a trainer, so selecting between alternative rides is an essential part of a good jockey –

you feel relieved when you are proved right, and very frustrated if the one you rejected wins the race.'

One of the outside trainers who occasionally put up Scudamore during last season was Neville Callaghan, a flamboyant character whose major successes are achieved on the flat. But he seldom runs anything without a chance over the obstacles, and Scudamore was fortunate to partner two outstanding juvenile hurdlers trained by Callaghan, Arnaldo and Royal Vulcan. They both won a sequence of races early in the season and Royal Vulcan was to form part of the jigsaw for the *Daily Express* Triumph Hurdle, fascinatingly complicated when Nicholson introduced his two main prospects for the race, Goldspun and Lulav.

Another trainer who began to court the talents of the prospective champion was the Somerset farmer John Thorne, and it was an invitation to ride his stable star, Artifice, which indirectly led to a dispute with a happy ending in Condicote.

On the last Saturday of October racing was scheduled for Kempton and Worcester. It was at Kempton that Artifice was entered, and as Nicholson's Oakprime was also booked for the card, Scudamore suggested he rode there. His trainer disagreed.

'David said he had three entered at Worcester and he wanted me to ride there,' says Scudamore. 'I was a bit annoyed, and a few words were exchanged, but it was not a serious row.'

'I insisted,' emphasized Nicholson. 'Business is business, and this was one of the occasions when I had to put the needs of this yard above the wishes of its jockey. I told him he would ride at Worcester and that was that.'

Normally Scudamore would have looked forward eagerly to the meeting. 'I consider Worcester is the best track of its class in the south,' he says. 'It is very fair for all horses and the facilities for spectators are good.' His anticipation this time may have been shaved by his lost battle to ride elsewhere, but as the afternoon wore on everything came right.

First, Broadheath, a four-year-old which Nicholson

had bought from Ireland after seeing him standing alone in a field, romped home in the featured pattern hurdle, priced at 12–1. His next mount, Spartan Clown, won at similarly long odds and the consistent Kintbury completed his hat trick in the handicap hurdle. The accumulative odds were 928–1.

It was the first treble of Peter's riding career and only the second achieved by Nicholson as a trainer. What made it all the more satisfying for the jockey was the fact that the horses he would otherwise have ridden at Kempton were all beaten. The boss had been right, and Scudamore was thankful.

Since Scudamore has invested in a cottage in Condicote, he lives only 200 yards from his trainer. But, as Nicholson says, 'We don't live in each other's pockets. Our working relationship is very good and we get on well socially, but it would do neither of us any good to be round at each other's houses all the time and constantly going out together socially. The strength of a business partnership is to keep it fresh and sharp.'

On the odd occasion that they and their wives eat together in the evenings, it is often in the Horse and Groom, a village pub at Bourton on the Hill, five minutes' drive from Condicote. A signed photograph of Scudamore in action hangs on the wall in the bar now, the relic of an evening of celebration late in the season.

The two usually travel together to race meetings, however, and it is then that the earnest debates on tactics take place. 'Nine times out of ten,' says Nicholson, 'Peter and I will go racing in the same car, and on the way we discuss each of our horses and how they should be ridden. Unless it is very early in the season Peter will know the horse anyway, but we are both always learning something new about them, and naturally the course and the opposition also have a bearing on tactics.

'In this department I expect Scu to do as he is told. If he rides the way I want him to, and the horse still gets beaten, then either our horse was not good enough or I got the tactics wrong and I will take the blame. But I don't expect my jockey to disobey orders and just ride the horse the way that takes his fancy. If I disagree with

71

the way Peter has ridden one, I tell him so. But I never cause a scene by bollocking him in the unsaddling enclosure. If the owner is upset, which occasionally can happen, I just tell him that I will deal with it, and I have it out with Scu in the car on the way home. I say my piece and it will not be said again. The race is over and forgotten then.'

Nicholson deviated slightly from this practised routine on Saturday, 21 November, when Scudamore rode his second treble for the stable in the space of three weeks. Once again it was an entirely sweet story, even though the venue was Ascot and the races concerned were all valuable in National Hunt terms.

The trip to Ascot took just over an hour on a wintry, muddy morning. Nicholson, as usual, went through the race plan for the stable's four runners, as he recalls: 'Sir Gordon was to run in the first race and I fancied him a lot. He had won on the flat as a three-year-old and been a leading juvenile hurdler before winning first time out this season. Our next was Leney Dual, a tough, staying chaser who I considered had a fair chance. I expected Josh Gifford's runner, Approaching, to hit the front about five fences out and if Peter could keep ours in touch he might go close. Goldspun was to run in the three-year-old hurdle and I thought he would win as he remained our best chance for the Triumph Hurdle. Our other runner was Kintbury and I gave him very little chance, but we talked through them all in the normal way. It was an exciting morning – a big meeting and some good runners. I would have been very happy to come away with two winners, but things didn't quite work out as I expected. . . .'

Scudamore listened patiently. He, too, was feeling the tingle of expectation which comes to a jockey with powerful ammunition, but he did not share his trainer's enthusiasm for Ascot.

'I don't like the place,' he says. 'It is impressively built, the facilities are marvellous and the racing is generally good. But the attitude of the gatemen is always unpleasant and frequently spoils my day. At the previous meeting there, I had ridden two winners – Goldspun and Captain John – and was standing in my street clothes in the lobby outside the weighing room, talking to Mrs Nicholson and Josh Gifford's wife Althea, when one of the doormen came up to challenge me. He knew perfectly well who I was and it was clear that I was not doing any harm, but he insisted that I should leave because I had finished riding. It was filthy weather outside and as I was discussing racing with two trainers' wives there hadn't seemed any point in standing out there getting wet. But this little man, very self-important, created a scene that was both embarrassing and unnecessary. The sooner that Ascot gets rid of people like him, who insist on taking their duties to ridiculous degrees, the happier jockeys will be to ride there. As it is, I know I am not alone in feeling that the atmosphere at Ascot is really bad.'

Scudamore's upset that November afternoon, however, did not concern the doorman but his trainer, who neglected his policy of saving rows for the journey home and made his displeasure known after the defeat of Sir Gordon.

'The Duke told me I had not ridden the horse properly. I disagreed, giving the view that he just hadn't been good enough to win. But there were a few sharp words spoken before I stalked back into the weighing room, where not even trainers are allowed. We were both still furious when the next race began, and I must admit I chuckled later when I read various papers praising me for giving Leney Dual a great ride. What the writers could not have known is that my determination had been fired by that row with David. I thought that things could not possibly get worse between us so I was going to give the horse the ride of his life.

'Leney actually jumped very deliberately and was some way behind the leading pack for most of the race, but I kept at him and eventually he began to respond. As we had expected, Bob Champion and Approaching went on about a mile out and had consequently been in front a long time when I made my challenge at the last. Leney Dual managed to produce his best jump of the race and I got him up to lead in the last 100 yards.'

Scudamore came back to a great ovation and a beaming trainer. The cross words and sour looks of less than an hour earlier were all forgotten now, and their moods improved still more before the end of the afternoon. Kintbury, who had been fancied by neither jockey nor trainer, lined up against some of the country's sharper handicappers and Scudamore had an immediate problem. 'Two of the field had withdrawn, which gave us a squeak of a chance, but Kintbury would only operate at his best if held up for a late run. Looking around the runners, though, I realized the same thing applied to almost all of them. Our only chance was Eddie, trained by Josh Gifford, and I was pleased to see him go straight off into the lead and set a pace for us. The trouble was, Eddie kept going and he was still half a fence clear with only half a mile left. Someone had to give chase and, selfishly, I didn't want to do it myself. We were all yelling at each other for somebody to go after Eddie and eventually Colin Brown did so, on Teapot. I stayed with him and won.'

Goldspun duly won the three-year-old hurdle, beating one of the other ante-post favourites for the Triumph Hurdle in the Irish horse Morton, and Nicholson was understandably in a mood for champagne.

Scudamore finally went home to his pregnant wife and, over a dinner with friends, considered what was undoubtedly the most successful and lucrative day of his young career. Any jockey who rides a treble at Ascot – and this one was in the course's richest-ever jumping card – has truly arrived. It was now very apparent to Scudamore that he could make a serious challenge for the title, if fitness allowed. That same day two of the other three races had been won by John Francome, and both men moved past forty winners for the season during that week. The race was really on.

8

At Home

Early in 1978 Peter was engaged to ride at a point-to-point meeting for a saddler named John Kington. Peter was no stranger to the Kington family, having ridden at gymkhanas and show jumping events with John's sons, Robert and Richard, but he was quite unaware, and probably uninterested in the fact, that they had an elder sister named Marilyn. Until, that is, Marilyn led up his mount that day at the point-to-point.

'It came as quite a surprise. Robert was apprenticed to Fred Winter and I knew him well, but there had never been any mention of a sister. But Marilyn and I got talking, and soon got to know each other. We were married two years later.'

During his two-year courtship Peter shared a cottage at Stow with fellow jockey Allen Webb – a typical bachelor home in which the primary devotion was seldom to housework or hygiene, much more to convenience and adequate comfort. Marilyn was a schoolteacher, specializing in history and religious knowledge at a comprehensive school in Newbury and, although neither was overendowed with spare time, the romance progressed to engagement stage and the wedding date was fixed for 29 May 1980, two weeks before Peter's twenty-second birthday.

'The first complication came when I broke my leg at Haydock in February. I had been going well, very well, and we had been able to plan for married life with a degree of confidence that money would not dry up. But suddenly I had stopped earning. I was also in plaster and on crutches for some weeks afterwards and there

75

was some doubt as to whether I would be completely recovered in time for the wedding.'

All was eventually well. The ceremony took place at Peter's old school, Belmont Abbey, headmaster Father Mark Jabale conducting the service. The honeymoon was a working two months in Scandinavia where, along with other jockeys such as Webb, Richard Linley and Andy Turnell, Peter rode in both Norway and Sweden and, on returning to England, the newlyweds moved into a tiny cottage in a hamlet near Stow.

'Another lucky break. The cottage is one of a terrace owned by Captain Macdonald-Buchanan. At that time he was senior steward of the Jockey Club, and also owned three horses in David Nicholson's yard, the link which happily introduced me to him. His son Alistair had also become part of the Cotswold House scene, having arrived at the yard to ride out, with plenty of polo and hunting experience behind him, but no racing. He had several falls, but learned and listened, and subsequently became as competent as he was keen.'

So for eighteen months home was a small rented cottage. Peter's career continued to develop between injuries, while Marilyn found a new teaching appointment, lower down the age scale at an infants' school in Stow. They were happy enough, but naturally craved more space, a property of their own and a child. All three were on the way.

'I had seen a house I liked, just down the road from David's place in Condicote. It seemed to have everything, including a garden and a stable block. I knew the owners, knew even that they wanted a sale to find somewhere larger for their own horses. But I also thought I had no chance of being able to afford it. Then, one day, I had been riding at Worcester, and had a phone call from the lady in the house, asking if I wanted to make an offer for the place. It was a big decision, but I will never make a better one.

'Knowing I had plunged beyond my immediate means made me work harder. I had a real incentive, and if ever a time came when my enthusiasm for racing, or just getting up in the morning to ride out, took a knock, all I had to do was think of the house and the money.'

One of the first things Marilyn learned about marriage to a jockey was that cooking is not an essential talent. Tall and blonde, with wide eyes and an infectious smile, she relates, 'Just occasionally, I have decided to cook something special for Scu when he gets back from racing. I spend hours preparing it, but invariably misjudge the time, so he has to wait an hour when he arrives. But waiting is something he finds difficult . . . he goes straight to the bread bin, nibbles at bread and cheese for an hour and then doesn't want the food I have cooked.'

This brings no indignant denials from the maligned husband, just rueful pleas of guilty. 'I never can wait for food. The problem is that I restrict myself to a maximum of one good meal a day. I have no breakfast, just a mug of coffee after riding out, and when I get to the races I will probably eat a sandwich and drink some tea – that will be lunch. Apart from chewing a sweet in the car, I have nothing else until I get home, by which time I am starving and have worked up my appetite so much that I feel I have to eat immediately. If I am wasting for a light weight within the next forty-eight hours, all I will have is a bowl of bran, but on other days I look forward to a plain steak and salad, or some fish – no potatoes, and very few vegetables.

'Mas complains sometimes, but she has now fallen into my routine, with just the one meal a day. It has its benefits as she is always losing weight!'

Peter enjoys the 'security' of married life, the feeling that he does not have to organize somewhere to spend each evening but can simply return home. He has never been one of sport's great socialites, for despite having to attend a variety of functions, he remains basically shy.

'I don't relax when I am in the company of a lot of people. The effort of making smalltalk with a group I have never met before doesn't appeal to me; some people thrive on it, but I am far more at ease with just a few close friends around me and if I go out at night, it will usually be with another couple for dinner, rather than to parties or clubs.'

Drink is as delicate a matter as food in a jockey's home plan, and Scudamore has not yet stopped experimenting in the quest to find the liquid diet which suits his needs and his taste concurrently. 'During the day I drink coffee, as I find it helps keep weight down rather than putting it on. But in the evenings, like most other people, I often fancy something stronger. I used to drink white wine, but developed a taste for it and found I was downing too much in a night. I tried mineral waters but found them boring; orange juice went down too quickly and just made me thirsty for more. So recently I have settled for having a couple of halves of shandy, which satisfies thirst and does me very little harm.

'I am always very conscious of my weight. If I have one meal early any day, I will want another. It is just the same with drinks. To do 10 stone, the minimum jump jockey weight, I have to work very hard and probably eat and drink virtually nothing for a couple of days. Sometimes it is worth it, often not, but at least I am fortunate enough to have a constitution that can take it. A number of jockeys, John Francome included, have made themselves weak and ill in the past through wasting unrealistically, but I have always managed to remain strong.'

Life changed course again in June 1982 when Marilyn gave birth to a son. Peter took some advice and the population of their charming Cotswold stone house rapidly doubled from two to four. The birth of son Thomas coincided approximately with the arrival at Ewbury Ring of a teenage home help, Wendy. For this addition to the Scudamore payroll, there were two reasons.

'Neither Marilyn nor I have ever been very tidy people – our minds are always too full of other things – and we found that the housework was never being done. If we had not done something about it, we would soon have been living in a layer of dust. But I was also advised that we would both appreciate the child much more if we had someone on hand to help.

'We found Wendy through one of those happy co-incidences – we knew someone who happened to know that she was looking for work – and since she moved in we have never once regretted it. One of the great things is that she knows about racing and takes an interest in what I am doing. She used to ride out, so has the right background, and it is good to know there is someone on hand at the house to take messages from trainers who phone.

'As for Thomas, he is like a new toy to go home to each evening. I am constantly amazed how much he changes and develops if I am away a couple of days. Like many others, I was never very fond of other people's babies and could not appreciate quite how different it might be to have one of my own. He is no tie – less bother than a dog, in many ways – and he has certainly made me a less selfish person, because I have to think for him as well as for myself.'

A regular visitor to the Scudamore household is a Liverpudlian stable lad called David Barker, who answers much more readily to the inevitable 'Scouse'. A lively and talkative companion, although to a southerner like myself his conversation loses something in the translation, Scouse has befriended Peter in recent years, but has actually been part of the Nicholson set-up since the mid-seventies. Little about him is conventional, especially the manner of his arrival in Condictoe.

'He simply turned up on David's doorstep one day and asked if he could have a job,' explains Peter. 'Any trainer's first question is "Can you ride?", and in Scouse's case the answer was no. He had never sat on a horse, probably very rarely been near one. He was from a poor part of Merseyside, and when he left school he had worked as a labourer for the council. The alternative was the dole queue, but he was passionately interested in racing, so he looked up David's address and made his way south.'

The Dick Whittington impersonation did not go unrewarded. Nicholson, although bemused about how much use could be made of a lad who did not even have the rudimentary knowledge of how to sit on a horse, showed the compassionate side which lurks beneath his surface gruffness. He admired Scouse's pluck and ambition, so he put him on trial. Seven years have passed and he is still there.

There is an endearing native wit about Liverpool folk which seems to override all other emotions, and David Barker fits the bill. He also turns his hand to various other skills around the house, not least the basics of cooking, and when in the yard he works diligently and takes the daily teasing with good grace.

'He learned to ride by trial and error,' Peter says. 'It was too late to start trying to be a horseman in the classical sense, and he will never be a good rider. Even now he falls off and everyone laughs, even the guv'nor, whose usual reaction to bad or careless riding is much less charitable. Somehow, Scouse is different, and I think the Duke and the other lads all appreciate that the place would not be quite the same without him.

'I believe he even enjoys the taunts and the ribbing of the other lads, because it means he is getting attention, and at heart he is just a bit of a showman. When he came down to Condicote he idolized Tommy Carmody, who at the time was stable jockey to the Dickinsons in Yorkshire. He will tell everyone that he has modelled his riding style on Tommy, although to me any similarity is surely imaginary, and even though Carmody is now back in Ireland and seldom seen on our courses, Scouse has not forgotten or forsaken him. We are all compared unfavourably with the great Carmody. Scouse took to calling the cat Tommy, and even our baby, long before he was born, had been Christened by him. I am not quite sure whether he persuaded us we liked the name, but Tommy he stayed!

'He drinks too much beer and, in the usual style of stable lads, he likes a bet. He is also a great soccer fan and, next to Tommy Carmody, Liverpool are closest to his heart.

'Scouse is amusing to have around the house, but also very useful, because he happens to have a photographic memory for the outcome of races. My formbook is like a bible to me and if, for some reason, it has got behind and I want to know what won a certain event, or how a certain horse performed in it, Scouse will reel off the details virtually without thinking.

'He lives in the lads' hostel at the yard, but comes down most afternoons and again some evenings; he likes answering the phone to trainers, taking bookings for my rides and telling them where I am. Unlike many lads, he has no ambitions to be a jockey, which is just as well, because he could never be good enough to ride for a living. But lads like him are the lifeblood of racing.'

Pregnancy meant an enforced end to teaching for Marilyn. She resigned her post at Stow early in 1982, with every intention of returning to something similar when the baby allowed. But circumstances dictated that her working life now took off at a tangent, and one to which she was in no way averse.

As she relates: 'At about the time I gave up work, David Nicholson's secretary was getting ready to go and live in America. She cut down her commitment to a few days a week before leaving completely, and the Duke asked if I would come up and help out with the paperwork just to tide things over. We got on pretty well, and I enjoyed the work, so after the baby arrived, and the secretary left, I took on the job full time.'

Peter was doubtful about the arrangement. 'At first I was not at all sure how it would work out. The Duke had become a boss to us both, and a friend as well, but business had to come first and I did not want any family loyalties getting tangled up in the running of our jobs. Fortunately, that has never arisen, and the team seems to operate together very happily.'

With a background among horses, Marilyn has never been one to fret about Peter's daily dalliance with the risks of the sport. 'I go racing with him a lot and don't often think about him falling. When it happens it can give me a nasty jolt for a few minutes, but it is much worse sitting at home with the race on television, just seeing him come off and then hearing no more about it.

'Now that I am involved in the yard and can take

more interest in what he is riding, I am even happier. Scu's job is my hobby and I hope it stays like that.'

As brutally critical about his own intelligence as he is about his riding, Scudamore claims: 'Mas has three times the brain I've got, and I wouldn't be where I am now but for her involvement. It hasn't always been that way – we used to row a lot about racing because she did not think about it the way I did and found it difficult to adapt to my professional outlook. But she came to see why it does mean so much to me, and gradually it began to mean more to her too.

'She now books seventy-five per cent of my outside rides and when I am away for a night or two she tackles all the messages and points various things out to me about certain races when I come back. I am often asked to go to Newmarket or Devon for a morning's schooling, but without Mas around I would not be able to desert the phone for routine riding-out.

'I often consult her about declarations and rules, which she has to be familiar with to do her job. She still doesn't know too much about the form of horses, but she does read *The Sporting Life!*

'Occasionally, she has put her foot in it, maybe telling me that a certain horse has won when she knew I could have ridden it. Then, I am afraid, I tend to bite her head off. But in most ways she is diplomatic . . . she never tells me when she thinks I have ridden a bad race, anyway.'

9

Family Matters

Michael Scudamore's rugged yet kindly features were contorted with exasperation. He pushed his flat cap farther back on his head and glanced down at the anorak and trousers, both waterproof, which he had donned in deference to the threatening rain. That was the one thing he had got right since rising from the lunch table an hour ago. It was pouring now, a constant sheet of rain whipping into his face as he stood in the yard and regarded the cause of his agitation. Then he had to laugh.

The Scudamores do not live only for horses. Other animals form a significant part of their day-to-day existence, and this was one of those occasions when Michael felt an overwhelming urge to abandon them and confine himself exclusively to the human race.

This particular afternoon had been set aside for the annual sheep-dip, required of every sheep farmer by law. In pleasant weather, and with cooperative sheep, it can be nothing more than a slightly exacting way of occupying a few hours. But in torrential rain, and with an obstinate flock, it can tax the most patient soul.

One beast in particular was being troublesome. She was older than the rest and slightly lame, but she knew what awaited her down that concrete passageway when the gate slammed shut behind her and was using every dodge to stay at liberty in the yard. Her clever tactics were providing a diversion for the other sheep who had so far escaped capture, and now Nicky and Michael were joined by a highly amused Peter in trying to trap them. Once it seemed there was no way out for them and someone – I fear it might have been me – commented on how placidly they were now heading for the dip. The words were scarcely out when old limper was off again, feinting one way and swerving the other like a Welsh fly half. Pandemonium broke out once more.

It was bedlam for the next twenty minutes. While a couple of bulls, apparently docile but chained down in their pens, looked on at the increasingly frantic scene, the three Scudamores – father, son and daughter – scuttled around the yard aiming rugby tackles at surprisingly fleet-footed sheep.

Marilyn, meanwhile, was standing on a grassy bank at one edge of the yard, flapping her arms every time the flock tried to escape her way, and trying to stem her mirthfully shaking shoulders long enough to hold her cine camera steady and immortalize the farce.

Even when they were all neatly penned, Nicky leaning breathlessly on the old wooden gate to keep them in, Michael's ordeal was not over. One of the larger specimens proved to be a more resourceful opponent than he expected and he met with no success as he tried to heave him into the dip. One final pull, and Michael slipped on the wet surface . . . the splash was loud, the curses louder as 12½ stone of Herefordshire farmer sampled the dip at close quarters.

This, of course, was all part of that odd affair called life's rich tapestry. That it happened to occur on an autumn day when there was no racing was by the way. The life of the racing trainer-cum-farmer is cluttered with these cameo scenes, even if most of them are not quite so uncomfortable for the boss.

Michael took it in the best of spirits, as one would expect of the most good-natured man you could wish to meet. He got in his car and drove the mile down from the farmyard to the house, dried himself off and set about the next problem, which was very probably finding a winner from his slimly stocked stable. Great jockey though he was, Michael has never made it big as a trainer; the Mackeson Gold Cup of 1974 was his most notable success, when Bruslee won at 2–1 in the hands of Andy Turnell and justified his trainer's still-held view that he was the best horse ever to dine out in the Hoar-withy yard. But that great day apart, none of racing's richest prizes have found their way up the winding, wooded hill, away from the river Wye and the main Hereford to Ross road. As a trainer, Michael has ticked over, but seldom beaten a drum.

The eighty-four acres of farmland are a compensatory factor, the sheep and cattle an extra source of income. But Michael makes no secret of the fact that he would love to feature alongside the Winters, Walwyns and Easterbys as the celebrated stars of National Hunt training, with large strings, owners clamouring for stable space and the problem often where to win a race rather than how.

Just occasionally it has depressed him. A few weeks back his yard was suffering its leanest period ever. He had less than ten horses and knew, was dismally certain in fact, that not one of them would ever be good enough to win a decent race.

'I took them to little meetings, spent hours trying to find easy races for them, and still they would get beaten. I remember several times watching my horses run from the stand at some small course on a lousy day, knowing they had absolutely no chance and wondering, Why the hell do you do this?

'Somehow I never got close to giving up. Oh, I might have come home grumpy from racing and told Mary I was going to turn it in. But I never really meant it, and I knew she never believed me. I am happy in the work, you see, even if it does upset me occasionally – and after spending all my life with horses, I really don't know what else I would do now.

'Training racehorses can be a heartbreaking business. I have had plenty of practice at watching bad horses run, but occasionally you get a good one go wrong and that is even more distressing. You get him absolutely right for his race, all is going to plan and then he falls or, even worse, breaks down. Then you really do think the job isn't worthwhile. But always something happens soon enough to change your mind and you carry on, living in hope that luck will change. Training is an awful lot of downs for very few ups, but when you are up it is the most elated feeling of all.'

Michael's voice betrays his homeland, his bruise-sculptured face conceals a million memories of riding days he would gladly have extended. In that time he became a senior partner among jump jockeys, a lively character by temperament but also a wise counsellor in whom many more junior riders, not least David Nicholson, trusted and from whom they sought advice. Nowadays his seat is nearer the back row, but he is not the type of man to harbour resentment about his lot. To describe his riding career in terms of cricket, which he follows with enthusiasm, his innings was long and fruitful even if he was unfairly given out while still playing well.

He was lucky to find such sumptuous property and knows it. His house, old and characterful, overlooks green fields, hills and animals. 'We tend to get blasé about it, I suspect, and it is only when someone arrives and comments on it that we realize quite how beautiful the surroundings are,' he says. 'There were no stable boxes here when we moved in. Some have been built from new, others converted from what was an old cider house, across the yard from the main house. It serves the purpose for the number of horses we have. But I do occasionally feel frustrated. Nobody goes into training with the idea of being middle of the road; we all want to be successful, and many is the time I have considered moving and trying to expand. But it is not that simple, is it? Our land is our security – they won't be making any more. And anyway, other than going to Lambourn, where could we live that is so convenient? We may seem very remote out here, but there are twelve racecourses within a hundred miles of us.'

Michael's routine is all that one would expect of a dedicated trainer. He is out of bed before six, which seems pleasantly bracing in mid-summer when the early work can be done in shirtsleeves but becomes rather more punishing to the spirit when ice has penetrated to the inside of the bedroom windows, the sun is more than an hour from a watery reappearance and the whisky which seemed sensibly fortifying a few hours earlier is now assaulting the temples like a rusty clamp.

'We start the feed at ten past six each morning. By eight o'clock we are riding out the first lot, up the hill from here on our own gallops. Back in around 9.30, swallow a cup of tea and a bit of breakfast and answer any phone messages then take out the second lot at a quarter past ten. Sometimes we have a third lot, if the yard is pretty full, but otherwise we are finished for lunch soon after midday and the staff don't need to report back until evening stables at four o'clock.'

Michael's staff is not vast. Barry Hills, one of the country's leading flat trainers, with an enormous string of more than a hundred horses and complicated security systems at his Lambourn yard, employs seventy people on a full-time basis. Michael, whose security is his own ears and eyes and whose string seldom exceeds fifteen or sixteen, has five lads. His daughter Nicky rides with enthusiasm and doubles up as stable secretary although, according to her brother Peter, 'she doesn't like writing'.

Head lad is Philip Turner, who has been in the yard since its inception and has suffered the juvenile antics of the younger Peter along the way. Christine Harding, Roger Roberts and Cliff Probert make up the squad, which resembles a family much more than a workforce. 'They are all local,' says Mike. 'And I hope they are as happy as us in the surroundings.'

Most of the Scudamore horses are back in the yard from their summer break by 1 July, four weeks before the start of the National Hunt season but in most cases several months before they will run again. Patience is the greatest virtue of the trainer, probably also the most difficult quality to master, as the natural impulse is to race the horses as soon as they look fit, rather than to wait for the ground conditions to come right. In the 1981–82 season Michael began well. Although running nothing of consequence before mid-September, he rapidly ran up a handful of winners, and the family celebrated in style the night Sujono, a Polish-bred horse Michael had bought himself, was ridden to victory in a novice hurdle by Peter.

'Obviously I like him to ride my horses when he can, but if David has a runner in the same race, or he is required at another meeting, that always takes rightful priority. I would love to be in a position to give Peter frequent and regular rides but I am not, so like other outside trainers I have to use him only when his commitments allow.'

But, for Peter, riding for his father is still a motivation in itself. He has never entirely lost the urge to live up to Michael's reputation as a jockey, so to win on one of his horses gives enormous satisfaction. Pride of place in the scrapbooks he keeps with attentive care is a colour picture of Nicky, as the travelling lad, leading in Peter after he had won on Beck 'n' Call at Ludlow.

'I always enjoy riding for father and as he has gone through some lean times, riding a winner for him gives me a special thrill,' confirms Peter. 'We always speak several times a week on the phone and I will ask him for his views on various other riding matters and on certain horses. I will listen to the advice of anyone who has knowledge of racing, but when it is your own father, with all his experience, he is always worth consulting.'

Like most caring parents whose offspring have made their way in a sport, Michael and Mary go to watch Peter whenever possible. If they have no runners of their own on a Saturday, for instance, they will often be found at the meeting where P. Scudamore features on the name board, unless he happens to have chased off into the far north in his quest for winners. Michael will dress in the classic racing gear of country suit and trilby, with his enormous, battered and ancient army binoculars slung over his arm; Mary, in soft hat and overcoat, will look as edgy as her husband looks content.

For Michael, the one drawback of going racing these days is his slight feeling of detachment. As a jockey he was a life-and-soul man, revelling in the togetherness of his breed and playing a full part in the socializing if, indeed, he did not actually instigate it himself. Now, he is classified as 'management' rather than shopfloor; as such, he is barred from the weighing room during racing. 'It is my one gripe about training,' he says. 'I miss the atmosphere in there, but I can see the sense of the rule. I believe the odd person would run between the jockeys and the bookies in the past, which might have been one reason for confining the weighing room to riders only, but the main reason must be that it is the one place a jockey can get away from everyone, including his trainer, if something has gone wrong. I would not argue with the logic of that at all.'

But while Michael ambles around race meetings, swapping yarns with old mates and sampling the odd beverage from the bars, his wife is in a permanent fret. Her nerve has never been strong when it comes to watching Peter ride and it is only through an oddly illogical compulsion that she watches at all. She has been known to lock herself away in the nearest ladies' room during a race and legend has it that she even pulls the chain on occasion to drown the sound of the course commentary. Mary will admit to none of that, but does say, 'I get extremely nervous, probably because I am so familiar with the dangers. I still take a great interest in racing, of course, and I study Peter's rides. It is worst when he is on an unreliable novice chaser – then I often can't bring myself to watch.

'I find it a little easier to watch him these days because it is obvious he knows what he is doing. But I still worry. The best part of the race for me is when it is over and he has finished safely. Naturally, I like him to win for his own sake, but I am much more concerned about him coming back in one piece.'

Tension is greatest in the Scudamore household when a jumping meeting is on television and Michael and Mary happen to be at home for the afternoon. 'No one could sit here and relax when Peter is riding,' says Michael. 'Mary is for ever coming in and out, wanting to know what is happening but not wanting to watch. One day last season she went out into the yard during a race to get away from it, but she then shouted through the window every few seconds, wanting to know if he was all right.'

Mary protested, but did not deny it. 'It is harder to watch on television than actually at the course,' she says.

'If Peter does fall, I see him hit the floor, just fleetingly, and then the cameras have moved on and I am left wondering how bad it was. Some of the commentators are very good and tell you whether the jockey is on his feet, but occasionally they forget and then I can get into a state.'

Mary Scudamore's anxiety is by no means unique. John Francome's mother is almost as bad, and seldom goes racing with her husband Norman. But to Peter the nerves of his mother are occasionally amusing, occasionally annoying. 'I do have to tell her not to nag sometimes,' he admits.

Even now, with a champion jockey for a son, Mary Scudamore would prefer him to be spending his time in another job. She even says so. Peter explains. 'If she gets me alone, maybe in the kitchen when I go home on a Sunday for instance, she will urge me to give up and do something with my A-levels. It still hasn't quite sunk into her that she is wasting her time.'

As the 1981–82 season approached its mid-point, however, Michael was proudly contemplating the possibility that Peter could be champion in his third year as a professional – something he himself had never managed in twenty seasons. But, realistic as ever, he pointed out the pitfalls. 'I felt he probably would have been champion last season because he had more rides than John in the last month of the season. But his fall ended it, and who is to say it will not happen again! I believe him to be capable of winning the championship, but it is a thing that only fools prophesy. He could fall tomorrow and be out for the rest of the season.'

Parental nerves for Peter pale almost into insignificance when set against the turmoil of a race-ride for his sister Nicky. It has not happened often in England – a handful of rides on the flat, followed by one over hurdles at Kempton Park, but on these scattered occasions Michael is as tense as Mary.

It was in January 1980 that Nicky, eighteen years old, blonde and attractive, made her National Hunt debut on the London course which tucks neatly into suburbia at the end of the M3. Her previous experience amounted to two flat races and one point-to-point (there would have been more if she had had her way), and now she was to ride Beck 'n' Call in an amateurs' hurdle. It was, ironically, the very same horse on which her brother had his first ride over hurdles, and Nicky did not disguise her dreams of emulating him. She had the bug badly, and Mum and Dad were not happy about it.

Michael generally watches Peter's races with a degree of equanimity; he knows the score and accepts the risks. With Nicky he was not so phlegmatic. 'That day at Kempton I could not take the binoculars from my eyes, but neither could I hold them steady. I jumped every fence with her and felt drained at the end of it.'

For all his gentle teasing of his wife for her sensitive nerves, Michael understands now because he has experienced it himself through watching his daughter. He makes it plain that he disapproves, not just of Nicky but of any girls riding over obstacles. 'They are the wrong shape,' he says bluntly. 'Their bodies were not made to take the hammer of regular falls, and that is what they are going to get. Some ride very well – Lorna Vincent is as good as a number of men over hurdles – but as a general principle I disagree with it.'

During her early years Nicky had shown little aptitude or enthusiasm for riding. Mary recalls: 'She was very nervous on ponies, until she rode Peter's Black Opal. He gave her confidence, and gradually she grew into horses simply by living in our environment.'

Once she had left school Nicky hankered after competitive rides. It was a natural ambition for any Scudamore, no matter the sex, and Nicky had begun to prove she was a capable rider. She rode out for her father each morning and did most of the other duties associated with a stable lad, in addition to acting as secretary and dealing with the yard's entries and bills. She got to thinking she might move to another yard, away from the confines of the family, perhaps work there in a secretarial capacity and seek freelance rides. But somehow it never happened.

Michael had always discouraged Peter from riding in point-to-points, sometimes bluntly forbidding him when the offered mount was considered unreliable. His views did not change now, and Nicky's urges to grab every available ride were kept sensibly in check. She did, however, ride a winner, and then Michael decided to bow to her nagging and give her a ride under rules.

Their disputes over what and when she could ride were generally good-natured. Nicky calls her father 'Bert'. He calls her 'Doris'. To an outsider their conversations could take on a mystifying note, but humour was never far away, and gradually Michael began to win the battle, Nicky began to stop nagging.

'I would never have actually stopped her from going into a riding career if her mind was made up,' says Michael. 'But I also made it plain that I would not encourage her. For a couple of years she was very keen, and went to work and ride in Norway, where she rode a winner on the flat. But there was no queue of people offering her rides in England, and maybe that, coupled with a very bad fall, cooled her enthusiasm. A horse fell on her once, a couple of years ago, breaking her collar bone and some ribs. It was probably worse than any single fall Peter has had, and although she was strong enough to come back and still want to ride out and school for me, she no longer badgered me to give her race-rides all the time.'

At twenty-one Nicky has discovered a social life which is as precious to her as riding; her life is contented and, as her ardour to risk her neck recedes, the same could be said with greater conviction about her parents.

10

Sticks and Stones

Just like his boyhood idol, Lester Piggott, Peter Scudamore has had whip trouble. Occasionally he has balanced precariously on the line between riding a strong
finish and treating a horse improperly and twice, in his
second season as a professional, he incurred the wrath
of the stewards and a financial penalty for what he now
admits were excesses of enthusiasm.

The relationship between jockeys and stewards is seldom cordial. So far as the jockeys are concerned, that is
hardly surprising. They are never summoned to the
stewards' room for a pat on the back, after all; it exists
like a magistrates' court of the racecourse, for offenders
and appeals, and the officials' attitude to the unfortunate
miscreants before them is often as welcoming as a cold
bath in February. Their manner is interrogative, sometimes suspicious, and Christian names are taboo. It
hardly encourages a spirit of goodwill.

Scudamore has high praise for the diligence and in-
tegrity of some local stewards around the country. But
only some. 'My great complaint is that they are inconsistent,' he says. 'Because of that, many of them cannot
command respect.

'The most disturbing thing is to travel around the
country and not know how the rules will be interpreted.
From course to course and from steward to steward
things change, and that does not make for a happy
relationship between the two groups.'

It was during the 1980–81 season that Scudamore ran
into difficulties for brandishing his stick too freely, and
he has no claim for injustice over the punishment. 'I was

being criticized fairly widely for using my stick too much and in retrospect that was probably true. The reason was not that I was naturally brutal or vindictive, simply that eagerness got the better of me. I never hit a horse which was not running and in my own mind I was certainly never cruel to a beaten horse. But if I happened to have a chance in a finish I sometimes gave my horse one more whack than anyone else rather than one less. The stewards were right to fine me on the principle that I had offended their code continually.

'The first time was at Worcester when I was found guilty of improper use of the whip. Ambition was the driving force here, plus the natural abhorrence of being proved wrong. There were two horses in the race I could have ridden, and as we approached the last, my "reject" was still in front. I tried like hell to get up, and gave my mount a harder race than I should have done, but still ended up beaten. My defence was that I had been trying to win, but I could not honestly argue with the verdict.

'I was less impressed at Uttoxeter a few weeks later. In a very bad race I felt that if I could really wind up my horse and ride him hard I would probably win. I followed the plan and hit him eleven times from the third last, but when he was obviously not going to win I put my stick down and rode him out with hands and heels. I admit that I hit him very hard, probably harder than I have ever hit a horse, but the vet's examination found he was completely unmarked. The stewards still fined me, and I felt then that I had become a marked man. After two fines I had to rethink. The threat of being stood down was now hanging over me and I could not afford to be hauled before the stewards again. I was still a shade raw and probably I felt hard done by. But I knew that the Duke would be the first to let me know if I ever hurt one of his horses, and he has never had to speak to me about the whip.'

David Nicholson confirms this, and ruefully recalls one occasion early in his training career when he overstepped the mark himself. 'I was new to the job and a bit too enthusiastic. We were at Liverpool in the days when their meetings were still mixed between flat and jumps, and I had a horse I really fancied for the final flat race of the afternoon. I booked Pat Eddery, who was then a very young jockey, and before the race I told him that if he needed to hit the horse, then make sure he hit it bloody hard. Well, he followed instructions, we won the race and went off to celebrate but, before racing the next day, both Pat and myself were called in and the stewards showed us the film of the race. It was hideous – I didn't realize, watching from the stands, but he had absolutely murdered the horse. The stewards asked for my explanation and I was honest. I told them that it was entirely my responsibility and that no blame should be attached to the jockey. They dismissed the case without handing out any punishments, but I have never given such instructions to a jockey from that day to this.'

The memory of Michael Scudamore goes back still further, and he points out that whipping was seldom an issue during his riding career. 'Very few jockeys were ever had up before the stewards for overuse – I went twenty years without one such accusation – and there was certainly no controversy over it. Yet I do not believe the jockeys are any harder today. I saw some horses given a real hiding in my day, and if it was a young jockey getting carried away then one of the older ones would sometimes have a word with him and say that it would get him nowhere. The stewards were rarely involved. I rode a lot for Willie Stephenson over the years and he was strongly against me hitting his horses – so much so that, win or lose, the first thing he always did when I came back to unsaddle was walk round the horse and check there were no marks on him.

'But they were not all like Willie. I rode for some trainers, and they had better remain nameless, who bluntly instructed me to give their horse a good thrashing. But it is a sad fact of racing that the horses who get badly hit are often those which can't go any faster and are already trying their best.

'Twice in my life I came back to unsaddle knowing that I had given a horse too hard a race, and on both occasions I felt a little uneasy about it. I got away with it all right, but I am not so sure it would have gone

95

unnoticed nowadays. The stewards are so much tighter about the stick now, because television and the media highlighted one or two bad instances of overuse and public opinion virtually demanded that something was done about it. No one likes seeing a horse knocked about, and these days the stewards have the advantage of film patrols to prove that a jockey is actually making contact with his stick.'

Peter points out the dilemma that confronted jockeys two years ago when the stewards launched what appeared to be something of a blitz. 'They became very tough on the stick, but also clamped down on jockeys not riding out their mounts for a place. It was easy to get caught between the two stools and for a while there was some bad feeling about it, but I believe the problem has largely been resolved in recent months.

'Jockeys know how far they should go with the stick. My own standpoint is that if it is necessary to hit a horse once or twice extra to win a race I will do it – and if I get into trouble for that, then the law is wrong.

'At the other extreme I have also had to learn to ride a horse out all the way to the line. Once at Worcester I was riding Grando King for Martin Tate and dropped my hands on the run-in when I might have got fourth place. Martin told me I had stopped riding, so now I go through the actions of riding a finish even if there is no chance of place money. It is good practice for the real thing, and at least no one can then accuse you of not trying.'

Scudamore's style of riding has won many plaudits but he will quickly stress that he still has room for improvement. Many advances were made last season, but the natural ability has been in him almost from the cradle. 'I am still learning a hell of a lot and I'm sure that I will be learning until I die. I never modelled myself on anybody in particular, but my father taught me a lot and when my style needed improving David knocked off the rough edges. I must have had the ability in me because he never had to give me a lesson as such. Just occasionally he would tell me things like "Bend your knees more" and I have followed his advice. I have never consciously worried about style, but I like to see good pictures of myself as much as anyone else does, and there is no doubt you can learn from them. The video is even better. If I have made a mistake in a race, won or lost, the video clarifies what happened. Once you are in a race you are not really conscious of your style, but that video makes you think about it.'

Style is most important from the last obstacle to the line and Peter says, 'Nobody ever had to tell me I was weak in a finish and I believe I have improved each season. Ever since I was a kid I could ride with the stick in either hand and pull it through, even if I drop it occasionally like everybody else. I believe the priority in a finish is to get the horse running out and feeling balanced. If he's not really running on one leg, then I change legs. But if he is going well I don't bother because it doesn't matter if you are Lester Piggott, if your horse is running then all you can do is leave him running.

'The stick is only for persuading the horse that he is not as tired as he thinks he is. Sometimes he may be really weary and you are working like hell to pull him together and get him balanced. Very often, at the end of a gruelling race over fences, it is much more a jockey's strength than his style that gets him by.'

One experience at Chepstow in the spring of 1982 broadened Scudamore's riding repertoire. It was Tuesday 13 April, the head-to-head with Francome was still raging and every winner was a triumph in its own way. The handicap hurdle had nineteen runners, Francome starting on the favourite, Royal Commotion, while Scudamore rode Born to Reason for Mercy Rimell. Peter takes up the story.

'Mrs Rimell's instructions had been very clear. "Keep the horse out of trouble, don't get him squeezed for space and he'll win," she said. So I decided that as most of the big field would come over to the stands side in the home straight, I would hug the inside rail and race alone if necessary. When we turned for home my horse was beginning to struggle and I thought he was beaten. I looked over my shoulder and saw Paul Carvill on Sea Cargo coming up behind me, with Paul shouting to be given some light. I pulled out to one position off the rail, ready to let him through, but he didn't come. Instead of dropping back in I stayed where I was, and after jumping the second last I caught sight of a different figure looming up at my shoulder – J. Francome. Stupidly, I had been looking after him and now I had committed the cardinal sin of letting my greatest rival – and the favourite in the race – steal up my inside. I was angry with myself and I also had a very vivid picture of the rebuke that Mrs Rimell would be rehearsing at that moment. I swore, as much at myself as at John, but he had gone to the front too soon. His horse began to shy, not liking being ahead, and without picking up my stick at all I managed to galvanize Born to Reason into a final effort and we got up on the line to win.

'John and I had cross words afterwards but I was wrong to criticize him. He had only been allowed through by my bad riding, but the race had taught me a whole lot more than that. I had won by riding a horse without resorting to the stick, despite the desperately tight finish. It gave me a new dimension to consider, rather like a cricketer who suddenly discovers he can play the hook after years of avoiding it. Since then I have tried this method of getting momentum without the whip on other horses. Some it works for, some it doesn't. But it is nice to know I can do it.'

That Chepstow race also highlighted the subject which probably provokes more weighing-room rows than any other issue, for when a jockey attempts to go past on the inside rail he is asking for trouble. It has always been the same, as Michael Scudamore relates: 'There was an unwritten rule between the jockeys of my day that you should never go up anyone's inside. We all broke it occasionally but everyone knew what the consequences could be – you might be put over the rail. I seldom got into problems, but I adhered to the same theory as most, which was that if someone did me today, I would do him tomorrow. You could not afford to seem the perfect gentleman or the others would take advantage. If it was only once in your life, you had to show your hand and be hard, just to gain the respect of every-

one. There were one or two villains riding then, and I
dare say there are today. You would not try anything
on with them or they would murder you for a pastime
– but everyone knew who they were and exactly what to
expect.'

In the hectic atmosphere of a National Hunt race
those jockeys who want to ride rough can often still
escape official attention if they pick their spot. But Peter
believes the amount of dirty riding which occurs now is
minimal, even though the bickering between jockeys is
as regular as it has ever been.

'Other than pinching each other's rides, which understandably causes the odd row, the main bitchiness in
racing comes from disputes over giving someone room,
stealing up the inside and a general lack of give and take
which makes certain riders unpopular.

'There are not many villains around now. Those who
wobble about causing trouble are very often those with
no real ability as horsemen, and they are never trusted
anyway. But I admit to one unsporting piece of riding
which was probably the equivalent of a "professional
foul" in soccer. At Newton Abbot early in 1981 I was
riding Rapallo for my father when Bryan Smart, on
Artistic Prince for Jenny Pitman, came up my inside. It
was a "him or me" situation. I considered he was wrong
to be in that position, so I spun him off the rail, losing
him yards and ensuring he had no chance at all in the
race. Mrs Pitman had a real ruck at me afterwards and
I would certainly have felt remorseful if Bryan had been
hurt, but I do believe one has to make one's presence
felt on the rail.

'My biggest row in racing resulted from a similar
situation, but one in which I can now see I was wrong.
Towards the end of a race at Stratford I was trying to
keep my mount close to the rail when Peter Haynes
challenged on the inside. He was going far better than
I was, so I should have let him through. If I had done
so, he would probably have won the race, but I pulled
across, shut the gap and blocked him. I was only a kid
and I imagined I had done well, so when Derek Kent,
Peter's retaining trainer, came over very aggressively

afterwards, I had a go back. He followed me into the weighing room and I have seldom seen anyone as angry over a race, so the yard may well have had a big bet on the horse.

'The crime in that instance was that I did not make room for someone with a far better chance in the race than I had, and that is the unofficial principle on which most of us work. If John Francome is going well, for instance, I would never try to go up his inner, but if he's going badly I would expect him to make room when I shout for light. Now and again things go wrong. One of my most difficult rides last season was Oaken Lad, a horse of Martin Tate's which has some ability but is virtually uncontrollable. I was climbing all over his neck trying to settle him but his only idea was to spring off into the lead. John was directly ahead of me and I yelled repeatedly at him to "let me through", but he refused to move. Eventually I got out and the horse shot off in front, but I was ready for a row with John when we went in afterwards. Fortunately, he realized what he had done and apologized immediately, saying that he had not realized I was genuinely in trouble.

'Another cooperative tactic during a race is necessary if you are so boxed in that you cannot see an approaching fence. Then you shout, "Bit of light – I won't go there" and expect the fellow in front to move across and let you see the fence, knowing or hoping that you will keep your word and not slip past him. Jump racing can be gentlemanly, you see, and it needs to be, for the sake of every jockey involved. If we all wanted to play it rough there would be more casualties than finishers in most races.'

Good jockeys, Scudamore believes, have an instinct for being in the right place at the right time, positioning themselves correctly throughout a race and producing their horse smoothly for the final burst.

'The priority is always to get the position you want, whether it is as the pacemaker, tucked in behind the leaders, or stone last. I try always to be aware of what is happening around me and I am either being unobservant or I have done my homework badly if I don't know the strengths of my own horse and of most other horses in the race. There is a knack, which the best jockeys perfect, of timing your acceleration so you hit the front unchallenged. The poorer rider will always find himself blocked by two or three others coming backwards towards him.'

Just as it is child's play for the practised villain to tip a victim over the rail, so it is a straightforward exercise to stop a horse in a large field of hurdlers . . . or so most punters will have us believe. Peter is not so sure. 'I have never been asked to stop a horse, and that is the truth,' he insists. 'Some people confuse this with the occasions on which a horse needs a relatively quiet ride – for instance, if it is his first outing of the season you do not go out with the intention of giving him a hiding to gain fourth place. Although one hears the odd rumour and occasionally sees something suspicious, I do not believe there is much that is crooked in jump-racing. If for no other reason, it is a foolhardy pursuit in these days of patrol cameras and vigilant stewards.'

If the stewards are only occasionally called upon to press the charge of not trying, however, they are kept busy day to day by objections from beaten jockeys, generally on the grounds that the winning horse (or one that was placed ahead of him) swerved into a jockey's line rather as a careless driver might cut someone up on a road. It is in this regard that Scudamore considers stewards are inconsistent.

'When you are called into the stewards' room on an objection you should have a very good idea whether the race will be taken from you or you will keep it. But I find that in almost every case I have no idea what the outcome will be. One day I might go across a strong challenger on the run-in, blatantly interfere with him and yet keep the race. The next day I might go across a beaten horse whose momentum is not checked and who would never have caught me anyway, but I lose the race. It makes no sense and it is very frustrating.

'There are some courses where the standard of stewarding is much lower than at others. Jockeys get to know them, and their characters, just as footballers will get to know poor referees. I do feel that stewards ought to be more professional and follow the guidelines more closely to avoid these ridiculous inconsistencies.

'It is an autonomous system quite unlike anything in ordinary industrial employment. There, if the management does something which the entire workforce believes to be wrong, something can usually be done to correct it. But in racing jockeys have no power against the stewards. The authority of the Jockey Club cannot be challenged.'

Michael Scudamore agrees with his son that stewarding standards are haphazard and adds, 'The patrol cameras have, if anything, brought an age in which there are more controversies over objections than before. I sometimes think the stewards carry their authority too far, but one thing I will say in their favour. Very often, they are decried for being made up chiefly of ex-army types with lots of letters after their names. But, just as in cricket, where the same sort of people have ruled for years, this type of person has a presence which commands respect, and that can't be a bad thing.

'There was one occasion when I lost my respect for them, however. I had a runner at Ludlow one day, a difficult horse who always got very worked up before his races. My plan was for the jockey to jump on early, before the call for mounting had been made. This would have been all right, but I made the mistake of not seeking permission. I was duly called into the stewards' room, quite properly, to explain myself, and I apologized quite humbly, promising that I would not repeat the episode without making certain the stewards were aware of what I was doing. Most of them seemed satisfied with this, but one virtually exploded and gave me the biggest bollocking I have ever had in my life. It was needless and silly.'

Peter accepts that stewards' decisions, right or wrong, probably balance themselves out over a season. 'I have kept races I should have lost just as I have been robbed of races that I am convinced I won fairly. But it happens to everyone. In April 1982 both John Francome and I made the long trip up to Ayr to ride on a Friday. John was involved in the first race, a handicap hurdle, and I watched from the stand as he won very impressively on a horse called Noddy's Ryde. I was surprised when I heard the call for a stewards' inquiry and astonished when I heard he had lost the race. It was a complete travesty, and for me to support John at that late stage of the season, when the championship could have rested on such a verdict, it must have been bad.'

Two months later Francome and Scudamore were summoned to appear together before the Jockey Club, along with their friend and colleague Steve Smith Eccles. The charge was that they had agreed, before the valuable Schweppes Gold Trophy Hurdle at Newbury in February, that if any of the three won the race they would pay a 'consolation saver' of £200 to each of the other two. They were each found guilty and suspended for six days at the beginning of the 1982–83 season. Peter explains: 'This sort of cash arrangement happens often in racing, just as financial splits are agreed in most other sports. The problem was that it appeared in the papers, and the Jockey Club probably came under pressure to be seen to administer justice. Officially we were in the wrong, and although the deal was perfectly innocent (Francome won the race and paid up!) the Jockey Club had received letters of complaint from the public and could not be seen to condone something which could feasibly lead to a more general form of malpractice.'*

* This incident is dealt with more fully in Chapter 14.

11

Racing Around

Jockeys spend more time in their cars than any other sportsmen. Indeed, with the possible exception of travelling salesmen and the certain exclusion of long-distance drivers, they are behind the wheel longer and more frequently than virtually every other British worker, many of them averaging something over 50,000 miles in each ten-month jumping season.

Very frequently a day's work for someone like Peter Scudamore or John Francome can involve upwards of five hours in a car, and rather less at the racecourse which is their actual place of work. Yet they can claim no car expenses, they pay their own petrol and, until very recently, not one National Hunt jockey had managed to obtain a car sponsored by a garage or motor company.

This I found puzzling, for while certain large dealers were willing to hand over a fleet of a dozen or more cars to soccer or cricket players, who used them considerably less and, in many cases, were virtually unknown names to the public, jockeys whose names appeared in the papers every day and whose faces were seen on television every Saturday remained in the commercial cold, snubbed by everyone.

Things began to change in the 1981–82 season. Peter Scudamore's remarkable rise to prominence, coupled with his winning personality, won him a deal with a Midland motor dealership, Warners. They provided him with a Peugeot 505 free of charge, and undertook to service the car at their own expense whenever he was in difficulties. Peter's part of the bargain was to agree that his name, and Warners', should be sign-written on the side of the car (something which a number of top sportsmen detest and will go to great lengths to avoid) and, in addition, to appear at a number of racing functions organized by Warners at their garages around the area.

Bob Champion, who, having recovered from cancer, won the Grand National to become a household name, was another to profit from commercial car companies suddenly awakening to the publicity jockeys could give them. For a time Francome was left out quite inexplicably, but when he pointed out in a Sunday newspaper article that he was still providing his own car, Renault obliged.

Francome and Graham Thorner, who has since retired from the saddle and turned to training, had met resistance from the Jockey Club during earlier, individual efforts to cash in commercially. Scudamore believes, however, that the time must come when jockeys are permitted a sensible and discreet level of sponsorship, maybe to the extent of wearing companies' slogans or motifs on their silks.

'If sense prevails, this can be done properly and channelled in the right direction. Flat racing does not have any need of it, because their jockeys are already far better paid, but the jumping stars are still largely anonymous and the jumping game as a whole is in need of all the money it can attract. Persistently turning away commercial benefits is short-sighted. People threw up their arms when Kerry Packer involved himself in cricket; they predicted he would kill the game, but instead he has made it richer. Properly handled, this can happen in racing too. Only this last generation of sportsmen has seen the benefits of sponsorship and some sports have shown more foresight than others. Still we drag behind, and my view is that the car sponsorship should be just the first step along what can be a profitable road.

'My car deal removes a lot of strain. The public seldom thinks about the amount of effort a jockey has often had to put into a day before he even sits on a horse at the races. If you are constantly worried about your own car, on certain days you will not be mentally alert to ride. Some of our day trips can involve about ten hours of driving. You need a reliable vehicle to get through that a few times a season.'

Peter does not often go racing alone, although he admits to sometimes enjoying the solitude. 'Life is pretty hectic once a season is in full swing, and the drive to and from racing provides a rare opportunity to think things over without having to switch your mind to other things all the while. The danger is that I will often start looking at my watch, then studying the mile boards and thinking to myself that if I drive at ninety miles an hour for the next hour I will be home. That is not only dangerous, it also makes me tense and I probably arrive in a bad temper, having been held up somewhere and missed my target by five minutes!

'On the long trips I prefer not to drive alone. If I am going north, perhaps to Kelso or Hexham, and none of the other jockeys in my locality is heading there, my father comes with me if he has a free day and we split the driving. That way, I avoid arriving home, inevitably late, feeling completely drained and in no condition to get up fit for racing the following morning.

'I actually enjoy driving when I know I am in command, and I do drive a lot better when I am fit and aware. But to us, just as to anyone else whose job involves many hours on the road, there is a constant fear of accidents, of an injury which could harm our livelihood, and at the end of a long day's riding I suspect the risk may be greater than when we are fresh.'

Scudamore's car fits the pattern of the majority which have constant use. It is frequently untidy, the front seat covered in music cassettes, the back a jumble of jackets, ties, papers and maps. He has developed his taste for music through spending so long in his car, and the stereo cassette player is now in almost constant use, spinning the large selection of tapes he has collected. 'They are mainly a variety of pop music although I do appreciate the classics. I have always enjoyed music, but it is only in the past year or so that I have been able to afford my tastes.'

A long-distance driver has his thoughts and his music.

Frequently, he needs something else – and the temptation is to nibble at what the doctors delight in labelling 'junk food'. For a jockey like Peter, this is a particularly dangerous habit, as sweets and chocolate can rapidly put on the pounds he has worked hard to shed.

'I try to avoid chocolate, but I will go through packets of chewy sweets and mints, mainly to give myself something to do. I also take a cigar with me each time I go racing. I hardly ever smoke at home, but I find I enjoy a cigar on the way home, and it also prevents me wanting to eat anything.'

To the uninterested public, one day's racing may appear much like another, but to the jockeys each card, and each course, presents its own individual challenges. Some days are inevitably more appealing than others, and if few jockeys suffer from 'the Monday morning feeling', they may quite easily suffer from the 'Southwell feeling' or the 'Kempton feeling' if the meeting of the day is one they rarely enjoy.

Scudamore's pet hate is Ascot, where the jobsworth doormen invariably make him, and other jockeys, feel unwelcome. But, that apart, he concedes that the course is among Britain's most testing and most fulfilling to complete. 'When I am going there I know I will always need a lot of concentration to get me round the chase course. From Swinley Bottom to the final fence is uphill all the way, and by the time you get there your horse's petrol tank is dangerously near empty. That is why there are so many fallers at that fence. But the rest of the track is difficult too, with three downhill fences which most horses rush at, and little room for error anywhere. It is a good track if your horse is up to it.

'Riding around Ascot, Newbury or Cheltenham is a great thrill on a good horse, but very precarious on a bad one. I don't turn down many rides, but for meetings on these tracks I will refuse anything in which I don't have confidence – it just is not worth the risk.

'Cheltenham probably attacks the nervous system more than any track except Aintree on National day. Even away from the Festival meeting, there is something exhilarating about going round the Cheltenham course on a good horse. It is a stiff, undulating track but you can gallop on it all the way, and the meetings attract very few poor horses. The fences there are so well made that a horse seems to sense they are there to be jumped, which is a great bonus in a novice chase!

'Although Lingfield is an outstanding course, especially when its usual conditions prevail, with soft ground and small fields, my own favourite race track is Worcester, and not only because I have ridden more winners there than anywhere else. All the fences are in the straights and on the level, so horses can meet them with confidence. To my mind it is the best track to send novices to, and that view is borne out by the number of runners the top trainers field there.

'Horses will often jump badly if they are going too fast, so the flatter tracks are obviously safer and, in a jockey's book, more popular. For the same reason, courses such as Plumpton, down near Brighton, win little favour with the riders. The feature there is a downhill slope containing a series of fences, and if you have fifteen runners in a 2-mile novice chase, it can be very hairy indeed. It would be unfair to single out Plumpton, because there are other courses with a similar layout, but there is no doubt most of the jockeys are more apprehensive about going somewhere like that and, likewise, certain trainers are loathe to send their horses there. No rider wants to get hurt on a small course and possibly miss some big-race rides, and no trainer worth his owners' money takes any unnecessary risks with his horses.

'I enjoy my infrequent visits to the north. Although there is no formal geographical split, northern riders tend to stay north of the Trent and the two factions only meet at courses such as Nottingham and Leicester, or at the major meetings. But now and again one of the trainers with whom I am connected will decide to send a couple up to one of the northern tracks and I happily make the trip if I envisage its being worthwhile.

'The atmosphere of courses can pass a jockey by as he goes about his business; apart from the obvious highlights at the end of the season, a rider's tension is pretty similar whether he is going to Fakenham or Folkestone, Newbury or Newcastle, and as he seldom gets in amongst the crowd, he is much more likely to form views about the place from its ground and its fences rather than from its patrons. But I do find that the northern racegoers are particularly friendly. They seem knowledgeable about the sport and certainly show that they are enjoying it whenever I see them.

'I particularly enjoy Haydock, which could be called the Newbury of the north as the track and facilities are comparably excellent. Ayr is another good course and on a recent visit to Perth even I was struck by how pretty and rural it was. The drawback, of course, was a car journey of six hours each way.'

Leaving aside the layout and quality of the racecourses themselves, and the standard of horse he is engaged to ride, two factors dominate when a jockey looks forward to his day's work and decides how much he is likely to enjoy it. One is the standard of facilities in the weighing room; the second is the number of 'bad' jockeys involved at the meeting. Between them, these topics can monopolize conversation between a group of riders.

Peter says, 'Some of the facilities for jockeys are awful. I realize that money is short at many race clubs, but no one should be asked to spend an afternoon riding in foul weather and have to come back to some of the primitive conditions we have to tolerate.

'In this regard, I think the northern jockeys suffer more than we in the south, as several of their weighing rooms are extremely rustic. But the worst of all is Fakenham, up in Norfolk, where the jockeys have to squeeze into a tiny room in an ancient building. The cramped conditions are bearable if you have one ride and the weather is good, but after two or three rides on a rainy day you squeeze back to your place in need of a shower – and there is none. Often you are tired, cold, muddy and irritable, but the best you can do to tidy up is wash behind your ears in one of the basins.

'Several other courses only have one workable shower, including Kempton, which stages a number of top-class meetings. At the other end of the scale, Chepstow and

109

Cheltenham have recently built new and relatively luxurious weighing rooms which make a day's work seem much more appealing. Cheltenham and Sandown also have a sauna attached to the weighing room, and this attracts a number of riders to turn up an hour earlier than they normally would, especially if they need to sweat off the odd pound. I would love to see more courses include the facility of a sauna, but here again economics must rule, and I would agree wholeheartedly that a shower is the first requisite.

'Jockeys obviously don't eat an enormous amount at the races, but if you are not wasting desperately to do a light weight, it is usual to have a sandwich and a cup of tea at some stage, and most courses look after us well in this respect.

'It is down to the clerk of the course to organize refreshments and in the main they are well aware of our requirements and try hard to meet them. It is not as if we are asking for three-course meals, after all. Just the odd place irritates and Southwell, a country track east of Nottingham, is the worst I have been to. The tea is horrible and plastic cups are left strewn around the room as there is never a steward on duty. It is only a minor thing, but it does annoy jockeys.'

Far more important than the needs of their stomachs, however, is the safety of the rest of their bodies, and Scudamore feels he and his colleagues are being unfairly jeopardized by the presence of incompetent riders, both professional and amateur.

'It happens mainly on the small tracks. At the big courses the major trainers dominate and their jockeys are usually accomplished enough to be sensible. But on a Wednesday at Fakenham, or a Monday at Southwell, one glance down the card in *The Sporting Life* is sometimes enough to fill me with apprehension for the day ahead. "Mr F. Smith" will have a couple of rides, although he has never been placed in a race during eight seasons of intermittent trying, and "Wonderhorse" will be there again, ridden by his doting owner "Mrs J. Brown", who will confide to you at the course that she has never yet got round on the horse "but he is a lovely animal at home and jumps all right, really".

'On most occasions this type of rider will also want to make the pace, so if you have three or four like that in a race, and your own trainer instructs you to sit upsides the leading group, you generally go to the first at a ludicrous gallop.

'I must make the distinction here between jockeys who are just starting out, maybe apprenticed to a good trainer and certain to improve in good time, and those who are plainly incapable of any improvement. My complaint is similar to that levelled by Barry Sheene after his recent ·Silverstone crash which very nearly killed him – in his case there were slow bikes and bad riders in his way; in mine there are slow horses and bad jockeys.

'The rule creating conditional jockeys, who claim a weight allowance and may have to give half their fee to the trainer, seemed a good idea at the time, but now appears to be producing far too many very moderate riders who are kept on at a yard until they lose their weight claim and then are dumped. Most of them try to battle on as freelances, but many are still incompetent and in those instances it would be much more honest if they had never been encouraged to start riding in the first place. Everyone has to learn somewhere, but in racing you need some natural ability and a good tutor to bring it out and improve upon it. If you have neither, you are in the wrong job and should be told as much.

'Amateurs are a separate issue but one which causes just as much heated debate. I exempt from all criticism a handful who are smart, capable riders – among them Jim Wilson, Oliver Sherwood, Paul Webber, Tim Easterby and Tim Thomson-Jones. Those professionals who complain that amateurs as good as these are pinching their rides would probably do better to examine their own credentials.

'But there is another band of amateurs who seem to ride purely for their own prestige. Some of them do not even dress properly, which brings no credit whatever to the jockeys' profession, but far more important is the fact that they frequently have little or no control over their animals.

'They are a danger to themselves, which is a risk they are quite entitled to take. But they are also a danger to the rest of us, which I object to quite strongly. If they want to ride competitively, there are hunter chases for amateurs only, and there are stacks of point-to-point meetings each season where they cannot harm the careers of any who ride for a living.

'National Hunt racing, by its very nature, is a dangerous sport and no one would like to see the element of risk removed entirely, even if it were possible. But the dangers could be minimized by better controls on the people who are riding around the courses each week.

'It is one of the very few sports where someone can compete at the very highest level with no proven ability at all. No jockey can succeed unless he is riding decent horses, but someone who consistently falls off, and on other occasions rides blatantly bad races, is clearly incompetent. It often does not need an expert to single them out.

'A bad jockey, professional or amateur, can "murder" a good one three fences out, ruining his chance in a race, and yet escape without a word from the stewards, who seldom interest themselves in anything which occurs prior to the second last.

'In these advanced days of camera patrols I suggest it would not be impractical to tighten supervision throughout races, and hopefully weed out some of the incompetents. I do believe it is time the authorities stopped ignoring a very real and dangerous problem and looked into the general standards of riding among jump jockeys.'

12

Winter of Discontent

Michael Scudamore was a working jockey in the winter of 1963, when Britain was imprisoned in an immovable cocoon of snow and ice for six weeks and racing became no more than a pleasant memory. Geoffrey Scudamore was riding sixteen years earlier, in what many old timers will insist was the worst and cruellest winter of them all. With motorways a fanciful dream and motorized snow ploughs still a thing of the future, transport to meetings would have been impractical even if courses had been raceable. The weather relented in time for Cheltenham on both occasions, but the usual programme of the National Hunt season was upset, and employees – trainers, jockeys, stable lads and all the essential ancillaries essential such as blacksmiths, box drivers and saddlers – found themselves dangerously close to the breadline.

Physical risk itself provides plenty of precarious moments for jump jockeys, but as their business months are confined to the winter, with a little sunshine tacked on each end, there is also the frequent threat that they will be left with no income for a period of days or weeks as soon as the weather turns nasty. No one will insure their earnings against the English climate.

In 1981 the snow came early, and by the second week of December racing had lost a brief, one-sided battle and had to be shelved until after Christmas. For almost three weeks Britain's unwieldy legion of jump jockeys, many of whom scrape only a meagre living even when the sun shines and the ground is good, were made redundant by elements entirely beyond their control. A few were fortunate, having subsidiary businesses to sustain them:

John Francome spent some time in his fish shop, Steve Jobar concentrated on his saddlery sideline and Martin O'Halloran increased his horse dentistry inerests. Others were cushioned by being paid as lads attached to a specific stable. But for the substantial group whose life is race-riding, whose wages depend on riding fees and winning percentages, the money lost in that period was neither negligible nor recoverable.

Three weeks of inaction were not going to break Peter Scudamore. But with a new home to be maintained and improved and a baby due in six months' time, he could not afford to be blasé either. But as he explains, 'It cost me a lot of money, which hurt, but I was much more annoyed by the simple frustration of being idle when things had been going so well.

'It actually did no harm to the Duke's yard, because most of the better horses had been run reasonably hard in October and November and the natural mid-winter break which the weather gave them meant they would come back fresh in the New Year. Horses are only capable of so many runs each season, and this was a chance to recharge batteries.

'For me it was not quite so straightforward. I knew that once the weather improved and racing resumed, my retained rides and outside rides would start to get crowded together, two or more possibilities running in some races, whereas in an unbroken season it is usually possible to organize rides more smoothly.

'The greatest frustrations came during the first few days of snow. Each morning I got up hoping and almost expecting there had been a thaw. I was still going through the motions of marking off my likely rides days in advance, phoning up trainers and looking forward to big races. So as each day came and went with the blanket of snow as thick as ever, I grew to be very irritable.

'After the first week my temper improved. The weather was quite obviously set for a while, so I forced myself to accept the fact that there would be no racing in the immediate future and there was no point in making plans for it. So long as I did not study the planned cards and think what I would have ridden and wonder

114

whether it might have won, I got through without too many black moods.'

Frayed nerves were not confined to the junior generation of the family. Hoarwithy, protected by surrounding hills despite its remote aspect, very often escapes the harshest of winter weather, but this time it felt the full, cold blast and for some days it was as much as Michael could do to keep his horses fed and watered; communications with the world outside were conducted by telephone only. A few miles away Geoffrey too was chafing as his farm was engulfed. Although he had officially handed over control to his son, it did not stop him fretting.

Stow-on-the-Wold, the nearest town to the Nicholson yard and a mere couple of miles from Condicote, is notorious as being among the most susceptible of English districts to bad weather. If there is fog around, Stow will be thick with it; if there is a frost, it will have settled in Stow. Similarly with snow and the bitter temperatures which accompanied and sustained it.

'I have never known cold like it,' Peter recalls. 'In Condicote the temperature dropped one night to twenty-five degrees below freezing. As in many other parts of the country, people were suffering with cracked and burst pipes and frozen water supplies, but we had the additional worry of the horses.

'It surprised me to discover that they did not noticeably dislike the cold. They certainly showed no signs of weakness; none of them lost their appetites nor their appearance. When we took them out though, it was so cold that their whiskers and hair quickly turned white, and in the misty conditions which seemed to prevail day after day they looked like ghosts in a weird dream sequence.

'Despite their apparent good health, it would not have been fair to the horses to take them out for longer than an hour each day, and it certainly would have been unfair to the lads. David had borrowed a field from a local farmer and all we could do was walk and trot the horses, then hack them around the field on the snow covering. It was valuable exercise, freshening them up

115

daily, but after a while I reckon they became as fed up as we did.

'If I had been in any doubt that stable lads earned their money, which I never have been, those three weeks would have put me right. I can think of several other groups of workers who might well have refused to report each morning in such arctic conditions, but the lads do it unfailingly and unquestioningly, even if their sense of humour is sometimes stretched. It made me reflect again on the relative pittance many of them earn; I know most genuine trainers would like to pay their staff more generously, but the money is simply not available. Perhaps if jump racing ever attracts and permits injections of commercial cash, some of it will be channelled right through the sport so that the grass-roots workers, the hundreds of cheerful lads, are rewarded adequately at last.

'While duty dictated that they were all present early every morning in the Duke's yard, my presence was more on a voluntary basis. I know a lot of jockeys decided that the weather was really too bad to achieve anything by riding out and took a prolonged rest. On certain mornings, when the ice had penetrated inside the bedroom windows and the only warm place was under the covers, I thought they were right and I must be mad. But looking back, I am glad I continued to ride out.

'There was nothing noble about it; I just felt it would do me more good to make the effort. The alternative, as I well knew, was to linger in bed for hours every day, which is a luxury I sometimes crave. When I was young I was never very good at getting up early, and even now I would list sleeping as one of the pastimes I most enjoy. But while it might have seemed a good idea at the time, I would have ended up feeling just as tired and I would also have sacrificed all the discipline which is so important in my lifestyle. Riding out keeps me fit, sharp and alert, even if it does seem an extra burden on busy race days. But during the bad weather it was my one contact with racing and I was reluctant to let that go.

'It was no longer just a question of falling out of bed,

pulling on a sweater and jodhpurs and cycling up to the yard, however. Getting dressed for riding out during that particular ice age became a complicated but essential business.

'From experience I had come to realize that the parts of the body most vulnerable to the cold are hands, feet and the tips of the ears, so I worked hard on wearing enough clothes to protect these three areas. Under my leather riding boots I wore a pair of thick, long Norwegian socks, and in addition I sometimes bound tape around the stirrup irons so that the cold could not be transmitted that way. For my hands, I find gloves are useless, but mitts are a help, and on a quiet horse it is sometimes possible to stick one hand under the front of the saddle against the horse's warm coat to restore the circulation.

'I wore woolly tights under thick, cavalry-twill jodhpurs, and then put on a vest, a shirt, a sweater and two Puffa jackets, one without sleeves and one with. I wrapped a scarf around my neck and on my head I put first a balaclava, then a riding helmet and finally a bobble hat. Under that lot, the ears are relatively safe from frostbite.

'Even under this covering of clothes, I could never say I was warm. My breath froze in front of my mouth and turned white against my balaclava; gradually the feeling drained out of my hands and feet. By the end of an hour – the absolute maximum session – I felt like an iceberg in urgent need of thawing out.

'The rest of each day might have appeared to stretch endlessly ahead without much to look forward to, but in fact I was seldom idle for long, nor wanted to be. My regular routine during the season allows precious little time for doing any jobs around the house and this was the ideal opportunity to catch up. I am not the most practical of men, certainly no do-it-yourself expert, but I plunge into home improvements with a good bit of enthusiasm when I have the time, and I managed to paint and clean most of the house during my enforced break.

'As always, it seemed better than doing nothing. Some

people are happy to have the chance of a few completely lazy days, but I get restless very quickly and find myself searching for a means of occupying the time.'

Christmas approached, the snow stayed. The last scheduled race meetings before the recess were on 22 December, but there was never much prospect of any resumption, and Scudamore, along with many others in his profession, was able to enjoy a longer and more relaxed Christmas than usual.

'In a normal year I start thinking about Christmas from the beginning of December, trying to plan rides for one of the Boxing Day meetings and, if possible, avoid any light-weighted animals. Having to waste for ten months a year is hard but acceptable; no one wants to maintain a strict diet on Christmas Day. I do think about Christmas and I look forward to eating the same sort of dinner as everyone else, turkey, roast potatoes and all. But if I was offered a decent ride on the 10-stone minimum, I would take it and sacrifice the dinner.

'It is one day a year, and I think only the most miserable of men does not go out to enjoy himself for a few hours, so I was very relieved that I did not have any light-weights for the one surviving Boxing Day meeting, at Newton Abbot. Although the Midlands were still covered in snow and meetings as far south as Kempton and Wincanton were early casualties, Devon had apparently begun to thaw and it really did seem that I would be back to work. In many ways, of course, I was relieved and could not wait to get back on a racecourse; in another sense I was slightly regretful that it had to be Boxing Day of all times.

'I followed the usual routine. The roads were now passable again in our part of the country, and some friends from Norway had arrived for the holiday. On Christmas Eve I drove up to my parents' house and then went to midnight mass, returning to Condicote in the early hours. A racing stable does not stop entirely for Christmas Day and I was at the yard at the usual time to ride out. Everyone, including the guv'nor, is normally in a good humour, and the exercise does us all some good before the inevitable eating starts. Usually, we ride out the stable runners for the following day, but this year there were none – we had entered only at those meetings which were already abandoned.

'I managed a substantial Christmas dinner and looked forward to Newton Abbot. We all drove down early the next morning, surprised that the snow really did end south of the Severn mouth. But after three weeks of waiting, it was a miserable way to return. I had six rides and the closest I came to any success was a distant third in a novice chase. The rest were tailed off or pulled up on the desperately heavy ground, and even the big crowd, the holiday atmosphere and the end of what seemed a period of liberation could not stop my disappointment.'

The weather had its say on occasions for weeks to follow, and a further blitz of snow brought things to a halt once again late in January. But the worst was over and Scudamore's season now really began to take off as 1982 moved into its second month.

13

Francome and Friends

Like heavyweights in the ring, slugging it out to the death, Scudamore and Francome traded winners as punches, and winced with each blow struck by the other. The 1981–82 championship duel became a classic, elevating National Hunt racing from its accustomed place to back-page news in the popular press. It was the cool, chirping champion, son of a Swindon builder, against his intensely committed challenger, the latest generation of one of jump racing's most famous families.

The distance between them was never more than a few winners as the season reached its peak, and both were stretching for the tape, seeking rides anywhere and everywhere, risking even more than was usual in pursuit of the prize.

For Francome the frantic battle had produced a resurgence of determination. Life, after all, had already treated him well. Since joining Fred Winter as a stable lad (his only previous equine experience having been as a boarder on the milkman's round in Swindon), he had matured rapidly into a master horseman. He had been champion twice in the previous three seasons, and three times overall, and at twenty-nine years of age he was keen on developing business interests outside racing – his flourishing fish and chip shop was apparently just the start of 'Francome Enterprises'.

But since that day at Fakenham, when he picked the style of a young amateur out of a crowded field of hurdlers and said, 'Bloody hell, who's that?' to his pal Oliver Sherwood, Francome had always known that there was a new threat emerging to his supremacy. So it was pride driving him on.

There were times during the closing stages of this epic season when Francome privately confessed he was almost ready to throw in the towel. The strain of travelling and wasting, and the growing list of bruises from punishing falls, began to depress him, and for the first time since I had known him there was no humour in his eyes and little cheerfulness in his voice.

But equally there had been occasions early on when Scudamore had doubted his own ability to match the talent of his opponent. Despite coming so close the previous season, when his head injury arguably prevented him extending Francome during the final days of the campaign, Peter still felt inwardly that he had plenty to prove. Francome clearly had nothing.

Scudamore's first day of self-doubt came as early as 2 October. 'I was riding Shermoon, a grey chaser of David's, and it was on his favourite course at Wincanton. It was obvious that our major danger in the race came from John on Les Kennard's General Election, which was thought of as a prospect for the Hennessy Gold Cup. We knew that Shermoon always tried to jump towards the right so, with Wincanton being a right-handed course, my instructions were to get on the rail and as near the front as possible. I achieved that well enough, but right in front of me, sticking to the rail all the way round, was General Election. He made all the running but I felt my horse had something in hand, so I just sat on him until we jumped the last, then pulled him out to try to get past John on the flat. We very nearly made it, but John had barely moved a muscle on General Election. Although some of the punters obviously thought John had just been casual, almost costing them their money, I knew otherwise. He had known where I was, how much ground I could make up, and how much he had in hand, and he won the race without tiring his horse any more than had been essential.

Even at these early stages of the season the good jockeys plan ahead, using their formbook to assess the chances of horses in races up to a week hence. Both

Peter and John have formbooks stretching back some years above their desks in the offices where their rides are mapped out, and they take great satisfaction from the routine. When their names are seen against a horse trained by an outside stable it just might be that the trainer has phoned the jockey, but as often as not it is the jockey who has seen the horse entered, studied his form, assessed his prospects and then telephoned the trainer to see if he can ride him.

In planning so meticulously, this pair are now in the minority. That is the view of Bob Champion, who retired at the end of the 1981–82 season. Champion was another formbook man, an avid forward-planner. But, according to him, 'There are too many jockeys nowadays, and many of them don't use a formbook at all. In fact I would be quite sure that a large proportion don't even possess a formbook, and that some certainly would not know how to use it. The same types will go racing for one ride, maybe in the first race, and then go home without watching another. It upsets me to see so many who clearly have no great interest in their job. Blokes like Johnny and Peter are naturally talented on a horse, but they add to that by working at the job, studying horses and reading the formbook. That is why they ride so many winners.'

The combination of formbook planning and natural ability certainly added up to one unexpected winner for Francome on 24 November, a winner which not only surprised but also depressed the watching Scudamore.

'We had both gone to Plumpton for a Tuesday meeting, on soft ground. It is not a course I like, and my rides were unpromising, so I did not drive down with great enthusiasm. A consolation seemed to be that John also had nothing which was likely to win.

'Every morning after riding out I go through *The Sporting Life* cards and form. I know most of the southern horses anyway, if not through personal experience then either by watching them or looking up their records, and I have a mental picture – usually fairly accurate – of what each one is capable of. I noticed that John was down to ride Integration, a seven-year-old chaser owned and trained in Devon by a farmer called Ted Retter. I was surprised. I had looked up this house when I had seen him declared and found that he had a dismal record. His formline was dominated by Ps, Fs and Us (the form abbreviations for 'pulled up', 'fell' and 'unseated rider') and, as I could see no evidence that he even had the ability to complete the sharp and taxing Plumpton course, I dismissed him from my mind. Now here was Francome booked to ride him.

'He won through one of the best displays of jockeyship I have ever seen. It was a 2-mile chase, the most difficult of races at Plumpton where those downhill fences are always a trap for all but the good horses, and Integration was anything but foot-perfect, yet John presented him so well at each obstacle that he had enough left to take up the running two fences out and run on comfortably. He beat the odds-on favourite by four lengths, and I was annoyed and dejected simultaneously – annoyed at myself for dismissing the horse's chance when John had plainly worked it out so well, and dejected because he had ridden such a faultless race. I wondered just how I was going to stop him being champion again if he was going to ride like that.'

This particular season doled out its favours equally, however, and Scudamore was to profit from Francome's misfortunes in later weeks . . . at Ascot on 10 February, for instance, when the margin between them had grown to eleven in Francome's favour, and the nearest jockey to them was Sam Morshead, whose thirty-one winners represented half Scudamore's tally.

Peter was on Nicholson's Sailor's Return, a horse rated particularly highly by the Condicote team. 'I could not think how he had been beaten when he first ran over fences early in the season,' says Scudamore. 'He finished second at Lingfield, but turned out to be lame, which upset me in one sense but made me relieved in another. At least he could come again.'

And come again he did, beating a big field of novice chasers at Leicester on 2 February then going to Ascot eight days later for a substantial step up in class. The bookies made him second favourite behind Fifty Dollars

123

More, owned by one of jumping's few Arab patrons, Sheikh Ali Abu Kamsin, and trained by Fred Winter and ridden by John Francome.

'There were only five runners in the race and two had fallen by the time we approached the last. Those left in were John, me, and Steve Knight on Run Hard. John was going better than both Steve and me, and there is no doubt I was second favourite as he took the fence, but he tried to shake up his horse and fell. Run Hard also hit the ground and I was left to come home alone. It gave me a great deal of satisfaction on two counts. I knew Sailor's Return was a very good horse, and it was like winning two races to pinch one off John like that. I took no pleasure from his falling, but he was well enough to get up, remount and finish third, so all was well.'

If that freak finish was instantly opportune for Peter, another incident three weeks later gave him far greater benefits in the long term, and but for his own mishap in May it could well have played a major part in making him outright champion. Newbury staged a qualifier of the State Express Young Chasers series on Friday, 5 March, and it turned into one of the mass disasters of the season. Eleven horses went to post, ridden by a selection of the best southern jockeys. But only five of the eleven finished, and two of the six fallers produced injuries serious enough to cause lay-offs for the jockeys concerned. One was Sam Morshead, stable jockey to Mercy Rimell and a close friend of Peter's. The other was Francome.

The carnage occurred at the twelfth fence when Morshead's horse, Celtic Rambler, came to grief and brought down Virgin Soldier, Francome's mount. For some minutes afterwards neither of them moved, and long after the race was over many sets of binoculars in the stand were trained on the spot where two bodies still lay, now attended by an ambulance. Morshead's injuries were the more serious. He had punctured a lung and could not ride again during the rest of the season. Francome was badly shaken up and had taken a knock on the head which automatically disqualified him from riding until the following Monday. Both injuries were of direct assistance to Scudamore in his bid for the title.

Peter recalls: 'John was due to ride Border Incident in the following race. Richard Head, the horse's trainer, was obviously looking for a jockey with some urgency and as I didn't have a ride, I made myself available. He booked me, and the horse won very nicely.

'John was very unhappy that I had been given the ride, and I could understand his feelings. In his position I would have felt exactly the same. But this was an instance when it would have been stupid and sentimental of me to think it immoral to take John's rides just because he was injured.

'I always feel sick when I see a bad fall in a race. My immediate thought is for the jockeys' safety, because they are mainly my friends as well as my rivals and I don't want to see them hurt. My next thought is thankfulness that it was not me involved.

'At Newbury it might well have been me. I was not that far behind Celtic Rambler when he fell, but managed to steer around the debris. John was not so lucky.

'I certainly did not immediately think, That's good, I can have some of his rides. In fact, that side of it never entered my head until I was back in the weighing room and someone said Border Incident needed a jockey. Then I had to be professional and go in for the ride, just as I would expect John to bid for my rides if something happened to me.'

Francome missed four winners over the next two days and when he returned to the saddle at Windsor on the Monday his lead over Scudamore had dwindled to just two – eighty-eight winners to eighty-six. Worse still from his point of view, Morshead's lengthy absence meant that Mrs Rimell needed a top-flight jockey for the stream of useful runners from her stable in the closing weeks of the season – and Scudamore won the vote.

'It was a great irony,' explains Scudamore. 'When I broke my leg two years earlier I was riding most of the Rimell horses. Sam took the rides while I was injured and got the appointment as stable jockey for the following season. So my injury had done him some good, putting him back among the winners after a lean patch, and although I felt very sorry for him I was naturally pleased to be the one who picked up his rides.'

With the pressure now fierce on both riders to continue registering winners at an almost unrealistic pace, BBC 'Grandstand' decided to film a documentary feature based on John Francome and show it on the Saturday before the Cheltenham Festival meeting. Hugh McIlvanney was to interview Francome at his home, with both Scudamore and Jonjo O'Neill being asked on air for their views of the champion's quality. Clearly they were expected to eulogize, but both were reticent. They said their pieces pleasantly enough, but it was not difficult to sense a certain resentment at the nature of the questioning.

Peter's reasons were these: 'John looked like being champion at that stage. He was still a few ahead of me, probably had a stronger hand at Cheltenham and plenty more to keep him going through the last two months. But we were still rivals, and to ask me to go on and tell everyone how wonderful he was is rather like asking Michael Foot to speak on the merits of Margaret Thatcher. Jonjo and I discussed this before we were interviewed, and he felt exactly the same. It was as if he was being written off as past it – when in fact I still rated him the equal of anyone – and I was being cast as the also-ran. So neither of us went overboard about how good John is.'

His honest opinions on Francome are far more complimentary than one would have gathered from 'Grandstand'. Although they are not especially alike as characters and live some distance apart, John and Peter have become good friends because of their rivalry rather than in spite of it. Chasing the same rainbows has inevitably drawn them closer and they both have sufficient humour to laugh at many of the situations in which they find themselves.

Peter recalls one particular day when both were riding excitable horses in a handicap chase. 'I was on Bamber's Security, an outside ride, and John was on his own stable's Prayukta. Both horses galloped down to the start with their heads in the air, going a ridiculous gallop, and it was clear we were in for a hairy ride round. When we got to post and had our mounts roughly under control, John grinned and said to me, 'I know where our mothers are now – in hiding!'

Francome's wit is frequently apparent in the weighing room, loudly joking while others are nervously silent, and pulling practical stunts on unsuspecting colleagues. 'He loves life and loves laughing,' says Peter, 'which makes him a great person to be with. If he thinks I am looking too solemn about anything he always tells me not to worry because I might not be around tomorrow – and that really sums up his attitude to life.'

A former junior show jumping international, Francome's greatest strength has understandably always been his presentation of horses at obstacles, but in recent years his strength in a finish has improved to the point where his fellow professionals will now admiringly admit he does not have a weak point.

A love of the sun, a liking for tennis and football and an enthusiasim for pop music are all facets of the joint-champion, whose career may well have been extended a few seasons by the challenge of Scudamore. He confesses he was running out of targets, that his lifelong ambition of riding six winners in a day looked no nearer fulfilment and that few other things could sustain his dedication. But in the final weeks of the 1981–82 season he drove more miles in the quest for winners than he had ever crammed into so few days before. He was bugged by the prospect of losing his crown to his new shadow.

Scudamore has great respect for Francome as a man and as a colleague – if they have the occasional disagreement, post-race, it is relatively infrequent considering the claustrophobic company they are obliged to keep on the course. As for Francome's ability in the saddle, Scudamore calls him 'confident and brave, which is why his horses are always presented so well at the obstacles. He gives them time, coaxes them through a race, whereas on average I am a more aggressive rider and occasionally hurry the horse into his jumping. Some are better suited by my style, others by his, but we ride plenty of winners because we can adapt.

'The older ex-jockeys will always claim that the men of their day were superior, but surely Francome is as good a rider as there has ever been.'

The Cotswolds are a companionable area if you happen to be a jump jockey. Not in the mainstream, like Lambourn, but still a busy and productive district for National Hunt racing, home for men whose livelihood is tied up in the mud and slog, the falls and fascination of the winter sport.

In his bachelor days Peter Scudamore lived with Allen Webb, a short, dark and dynamic jockey who has emerged from some bleak days to a more settled existence as retained rider to trainer Kim Bailey.

Webb and Scudamore mixed socially and business-wise, with a handful of Cotswold colleagues, notably John Suthern, Paul Carvill and Robin Dickin. Every one of them had at some stage ridden for David Nicholson. Every one had experienced the downs and the depression which inevitably come with such a precarious life-style; but every one had also retained his sense of humour.

It was just as well that they had, for circumstances were not always kind. Into the life of every jockey, so the averages decree, must come one fall in every eight or ten rides; the lucky ones have a winner or two thrown into that period too. But a few seasons ago Peter recalls a day at Leicester when it seemed the fates had conspired against him and his friends.

'I was still an amateur in those days; John and Robin were in the Duke's yard and Webby was riding as a freelance. We regularly shared a car when we were all going to the same meeting, and there was the usual feeling of anticipation on the way to racing – we all felt we could ride a winner, of course.

'The day was rotten from start to finish. Robin turned over in the novice chase, a dreadful fall, and ended up in hospital. I came off on the flat and cracked a bone in my wrist. John was beaten on his mounts, yet could have gone elsewhere to ride two for John Bridger, both of which won.

'We were together in the weighing room afterwards, the three of us, minus Robin, and somehow we still managed to laugh about it all. Webby was crowing that he was the only one who had come through the day unscathed but at that moment John Suthern sighed, moaned, "What a bloody awful day," and sat down heavily on the bench, crushing Webby's false teeth which he had left out to pack. It cost Allen £80 and he ended up worse off than any of us!'

Paul Carvill was not present that day but has suffered more than his share of bad times. Slightly older than Scudamore and another native of Condicote, Carvill had a wretched season in 1981–82, the sort when winners are as frequent as snowstorms in July. But on the May Day Bank Holiday, a mere month from the end of jumping, he at last enjoyed a little luck.

Peter explains: 'Like me, Paul is a Catholic, and because he is serious about his religion, he is nicknamed "The Pope" and endlessly ribbed in a good-humoured way. He takes it all in the right spirit and is very good company; he is also a good jockey, but needs better horses to change his career. On this particular day he was bound for Kelso where he was to ride the following day, but needed to make a detour to pick up his tack at Towcester. He got there to be told that Robert Hughes had not arrived from his home in Epsom – Paul was offered the spare ride on Gazaan, a useful hurdler, and duly won. The race was over when Hughes eventually arrived, naturally annoyed to have missed a winner. Someone asked him why he was so late and Robert replied, "I was held up in the crowds going to see the Pope." Nobody laughs at Paul's nickname any more, because he can always tell that story.'

Suthern, at thirty-one, is the oldest member of Scudamore's Cotswold social group and, according to Peter, 'Is always being teased, both about his age and his eyesight. He has not been allowed to forget that a pressman recently wrote with a degree of surprise that "John Suthern has not given up. . . ." But John and Allen are both brave and tremendously strong in a finish. The way they ride from the last to the line is an example to any aspiring youngster.'

Although these local friends are obviously closest to Scudamore, the jockeys and their weighing-room brotherhood are such that most see each other as mates. Fall-outs occur, grudges are occasionally built up, but these are the exceptions to an otherwise happy rule.

On his infrequent ventures north Peter enjoys seeing the ability of riders not often on show in his domain. 'Jonjo is clearly the best and a match for anyone in the country. Every aspect of his riding is outstanding; he has the instinct to time a run perfectly, and when I was laid up with a broken leg I studied videos of his riding and learned a lot. To come back, as he did, a year later from such a terrible leg injury was the mark of a very tough guy, and I would rate him equally as talented as John Francome.'

But if Jonjo and his northern colleagues like Ridley Lamb, Neale Doughty and Colin Hawkins are all extremely accomplished, the Scudamore eye is trained far more often on Francome and the southerners, of whom Hywel Davies and Steve Smith Eccles have recently become the most successful.

'Steve is a great mate of John Francome and often holidays with him. Just like John, he is a bouncy character, but the thing which first made me like him was the fact that he treats everyone in the weighing room the same. There are some jockeys who scarcely speak to a young rider until he has proved himself with a few winners, but Steve chatters and jokes with everyone from the newest apprentice to the most senior professional.

'He has had spells with Nicky Henderson and Alan Jarvis but went freelance in 1981 and is really the only successful southerner without a home stable. He is second jockey to the Duke, but opportunities are limited for him there so he uses his contacts and his energy, not to mention his ability, to attract rides from a great variety of other trainers around the country.

'He lives in flat-racing country at Newmarket so spends a lot of time in his car, admits to "driving it like stink", and is great fun socially. My most striking memory of him comes from one of his home courses at Huntingdon, however, when he won on Harry Hotspur, a difficult ride, simply by sticking like to glue to the rails all the way round. If he had come off at all, I believe I would have beaten him because I always felt I was going better, but I just could not get through. It was Steve at his tenacious best and one of the best individual rides I have ever seen a jockey give.

'Hywel and I are of similar age and similar mind. We both think very deeply about our rides and probably get too intense for our own good now and again. But ever since we both started making our way, Hywel as an apprentice with Josh Gifford and me as an amateur, we have been close friends. I now rate him one of the best around – and so does he! Another of our traits is that we both imagine we are brilliant, and talk to each other for hours on end about how well we managed to get this horse or that around a difficult track.

'In the weighing room Hywel is for ever telling appalling jokes and then roaring with laughter while everyone else stands with blank faces. He is also gullible, a prime target for teasing, and I often get him going by telling him I have been schooling certain horses for one of his trainers.'

In many ways, a gathering of jump jockeys is little different from a gathering of any other particular breed of sportsmen. The humour can be crude, the language cruder, the conversation ranging from sex to sport and back again with an occasional stop on the way. But there is something different; it is the bond of being together in a sport when danger presents itself up to twenty times in five or six minutes, and where everyone, some time, will feel the impact of a horse's shoe and smell the antiseptic of a hospital ward. In jump racing, good friends are often more important than good rides; you need both to be a star.

14

Big Race Days

The appetizers and hors d'oeuvres of the jumping season occupy six months and see autumn turn to winter and winter nearly to spring. Then the main course has to be digested in a matter of eight weeks, the stage switching rapidly from Newbury in the south, to Cheltenham in the Cotswolds and finally to Liverpool in the northwest. These three meetings attract the biggest crowds, the biggest bets and, for the jockeys, the most attention. With that comes more tension, more anticipation and, for the fortunate few, the fattest purses of the winter slog.

In 1982 the first of these spotlighted occasions fell on 13 February with the running of the Schweppes Hurdle, traditionally the most open and hotly contested handicap of the year, a cavalry charge of around thirty horses over 2 miles. A month later, in similar bottomless mud at Cheltenham, the Festival went ahead despite threats of abandonment, and Peter Scudamore was able to ride his beloved Broadsword in the biggest race of his young life. Then, on 4 April, with spring sunshine trying hard to shine on Merseyside, thirty-nine runners went to post for what many believed would be the final running of the most famous steeplechase in the world.

Scudamore tells his own story of these three big-race days:

The Schweppes Handicap Hurdle

'Nobody likes being labelled a cheat, either directly or by inference – but that is my main memory of the

132

Schweppes last year. I finished only sixth, yet I ended in front of the Jockey Club disciplinary committee, along with John Francome and Steve Smith Eccles.

'To most people the charge against us may have seemed petty. But it was real enough to us when we were banned from the first week of the 1982–83 season – found guilty of what some may have construed as trying to rig the outcome of the race. What really happened was as innocent as a footballer buying one of the opposition a drink after the game, yet the three of us have come away from that hearing with the equivalent of an endorsement in a driving licence, and it is not a pleasant feeling.

'The build-up to the Schweppes is always one of the keenest in a season because so many horses are fancied, and as David Nicholson did not have a runner it was up to me to act as a freelance and obtain the best possible ride for myself. Nicky Henderson, a young and successful trainer in Lambourn, approached me for one of his two entries and on perusing the formbook I came to the conclusion that they both had a very reasonable chance. Steve Smith Eccles, who was once Nick's stable jockey, had the choice of the pair and opted for Mount Harvard, but I was not at all disappointed to be left with The Tsarevich. His best run the previous season had been a second in the final of the Panama Hurdle – I had ridden the Irish-trained winner, but The Tsarevich ran me close. I knew he was useful.

'My own feeling was that Gaye Chance would win. Tipping is a mug's game in a race like the Schweppes, but along with Ekbalco, a brilliant horse which needs holding up to the last possible moment, Gaye Chance represented the highest class in the field. My view was certainly not altered when, only a couple of days before the race, trainer Paul Kelleway booked John Francome to ride his Donegal Prince. A fair horse on the flat, he had shown nothing of great note over hurdles and you could not logically fancy him, especially as John had to put up about 4 pounds overweight.

'Steve and I both thought we had a chance, and as we were riding for the same stable there was naturally an added incentive existing to outdo each other. I got the impression that John did not fancy his horse, which may have been why he suggested a split of winnings if any of us won. It was the type of thing that is often mooted when jockeys, or other sportsmen for that matter, sit around discussing a forthcoming event. It is a known fact that Test cricket teams have divided up the cash after one-day internationals and I have no doubt something similar is done in many other sports. There is nothing intentionally devious about it and it certainly does not hint at collusion – which in most cases is simply not practicable anyway.

'John's idea was that if any of the three of us should win the race, he should pay each of the other two £200, which amounts to around ten per cent of the jockey's winning cut from the Schweppes. I suspect Steve and I both privately thought we had more chance of paying out than John, but we agreed happily enough. It was nothing new, after all.

'I thought no more about it, because it seemed such a trivial thing – more a conversation-filler than anything else. Very often before a race a jockey whose horse needs to be taken along at a good gallop will ask for a volunteer to make the pace and maybe throw in a tenner as the bait. He is usually accommodated. And at the end of a race a jockey who is not in contention for places, but jumps the last upsides another, will often agree, virtually in mid-air, on a race to the line for a fiver or a gin-and-tonic just to sustain some sporting interest. If anyone can detect something wrong in these habits I would be surprised – and John, Steve and I considered the Schweppes saver in the same light.

'If we could fix the Schweppes with £200 stakes we would all be millionaires. Races like that just cannot be bent – it isn't possible. But, more relevant, the prestige of winning the race meant much more to me, and I imagine to Steve and John too, than the lure of money. Of course the cash is important, but this was one of the major races in the calendar and none of us had won it. If someone had assured me that he was having a word with the Almighty's aides and it would cost me £500 to win the race, I would happily have paid up.

'Race day was bright and sunny, but torrential overnight rain had turned the course into a bog. The previous day the ground had been almost ideal, and my two winners had included a convincing success on Lulav in the Stroud Green Hurdle. Now the going was officially heavy and rode like it. Not that I had experienced it for too long before the Schweppes – my one early ride, On a Cloud, in the first, had capsized at the second hurdle. It was the jockey's nightmare, a fall before a major event, but I got up with nothing more serious than a few bruises and a lot of mud to contemplate as I began the long walk back across the course to the weighing room. John won the second race on News King, which did my mood no good at all, but as we hacked down to the 2-mile start twenty minutes later I was thinking of nothing but winning the Schweppes. Certainly odd payouts of £200 were furthest from my mind.

'The pace of the Schweppes is usually extremely quick and as I looked round at the rest of the field, all twenty-six of them, I wondered who would be setting the murderous gallop this time. But I was surprised to find that nobody seemed keen to make it; in fact for the first half of the race John was in front on Donegal Prince and I was tucked in just behind him. Frankly I felt neither of us was looking comfortable and, as we approached the sixth and I went to take it up, our side stake crossed my mind. I yelled across at John, 'My £200 isn't looking too clever, how about yours?' I didn't catch his reply but he was already hard at work on Donegal Prince and I felt that my pre-race suspicions about the horse were being proved correct.

'I was still ahead at the second last and John seemed to be nowhere. The pace had quickened dramatically and I knew someone was going to come past me. I thought fleetingly it was sure to be Gaye Chance or Ekbalco, but to my surprise it was Francome, urging Donegal Prince ahead again.

'Over the last two more had gone past, Ekbalco, and Steve on Mount Harvard, and while I drove out The

135

Tsarevich to try to obtain the best possible placing, I was aware of tremendous excitement in the crowd and a blanket finish up ahead of me. My first impression, admittedly judged from a poor position, was that Ekbalco had got up to win, and as we walked the horses back John confided the same fear. Steve just didn't know.

'But the photo showed that Donegal Prince had held on by a head, with Mount Harvard a further neck away in third. Celebratory chatter and backslapping followed in the weighing room, with Steve and John conducting their usual double act of witty cross-talk and leg-pulling. I could not be disappointed with my horse, he had finished sixth and run a game race, and I was pleased for John despite the fact that it took him one more winner away from me.

'Neither Steve nor I mentioned the money. I had certainly forgotten all about it and would probably not have given it another thought. But John is a man of his word and before we left the course that evening he promised to pay us both. It was some consolation for a day without a winner, and I expected to hear no more about it.

'I travelled home with the Duke that night, and the car radio was tuned into the sports show as usual. John was interviewed, and in a lighthearted voice he told how he had already given away £400 of his winnings, going on to tell the story of our split. John clearly saw it as rather funny that he should have had to pay out, and neither the Duke nor I saw anything dangerous in his relating the tale. After all, he and Steve had been combatants in one of the closest Schweppes finishes for years and I had not been far behind. No one could accuse us of cheating, could they? On that, it seems, we were wrong.

'Three months passed, a lot of major races went under the bridge and the Schweppes had long since ceased to be a weighing-room talking point. The season was almost over in fact, when I had a call from the Racecourse Security Services. A voice informed me that they were investigating alleged payments between jockeys after the Schweppes Hurdle, and that they would like to interview me as soon as possible. I was amazed, first, at the fact that it was being inquired into at all and, second, that it was so long after the event. But I thought nothing would come of it and fixed a date for a visit.

'The security official who arrived at my door certainly had an interrogative manner. So much so that I began to suspect he was conducting a witch-hunt, an opinion I later dismissed. He kept using the words "bet" and "hanky-panky". I told him that it was wrong to construe what we had arranged as a bet and that there was never any intention of hanky-panky. Was he suggesting that we could rig a race of twenty-seven runners just so that John could win it and pay us £200?

'I wondered later whether I should have denied the whole thing had happened. If I had known the investigations were to be so deep, it might have seemed an easy way out – but then John's broadcast banter about the side stake had indicted all three of us. He had also told the story in his newspaper column in the *Sun*.

'The summons duly arrived. We were to appear at Portman Square in front of the Jockey Club's Disciplinary Committee. Only then, I think, did any of us realize quite how serious our position was. The options open to the committee, should they find us guilty, included withdrawing our licences to ride. With that knowledge, we hired a solicitor, Mr Matthew McCloy, to defend us.

'The hearing was delayed due to John's holiday in Ireland but was finally set for two weeks before the start of the new season. The three of us met in the lounge of the plush Churchill Hotel, opposite the Jockey Club headquarters; we were all smartly dressed in suits, and although the customary joking did not entirely dry up, it was tinged with nervousness.

'We knew we had done nothing immoral. But we also knew we had broken the letter of the law, and this was underlined to us by Mr McCloy when he arrived at the hotel. He said he could see no alternative for the committee but to ban us, and asked us whether we wanted him to put up a fight. As we had hired him, there seemed no point in giving up without some defence, so we instructed him to plead on the lines that our financial arrangement was no different to the common practice, equally illegal under strict interpretation of the rules, by which a winning jockey will give a party or buy champagne after a big race. It was a theory which increasingly convinced us that we were in the right, but Steve in particular was amusingly bent on predicting doom. "We're all for the chop," he kept saying, making vigorous chopping motions with his hand. I must admit I was pretty tense about it all by then, and yet it seemed so ridiculous.

'Mr McCloy put our case well and we were given a full and fair "trial". But they did not accept our reasoning and we were banned for one week, coinciding with the start of the season and also taking in races in Ireland and Norway that I had planned to travel to.

'I was annoyed more than anything else. Their judgement was officially quite correct as we could not deny we had committed an offence against their rules. So I could understand the punishment meted out and even appreciated that it could have been harsher. But still, it somehow seemed comical.

'Bringing the case so long after the event was an absurdity and could only mean that they had come under pressure, either from public complaints about this apparent malpractice, or from a person or persons within the hierarchy who objected to the deal being made public. Nevertheless, I thought a fine would have been more appropriate for something which was so obviously done in innocent fun, and the whole tangled affair did nothing to increase my respect for the Jockey Club.'

Cheltenham

It takes only a matter of seconds in racing for months of expectation to be dashed, and for dreams to die. Cheltenham, on a bleak, cold Tuesday in March, was the setting for the Condicote dreams to be lived out, with the stable idol Broadsword taking on the best hurdlers from each side of the Irish Sea and bidding to become the first five-year-old to win the Champion Hurdle since the great Night Nurse in 1976.

David Nicholson was glowing with confidence. Even Scudamore, customarily reserved to the point of caution in all his judgements, believed 'Broady' could do it. Yet he failed, and in the most unpredictable of fashions, beaten by a 40–1 long shot when all the fancied contenders had been left behind.

In the few minutes it took Scudamore to turn his horse around and walk him back to unsaddle, the anguish of an ambition denied was paraded across his features. I have never seen him look so dejected. Nicholson, too, found it hard to entirely conceal his disappointment, but later, a safe distance from emotion, he was philosophical about a Festival that had promised so much and produced so little.

'I went to Cheltenham with a strong hand but didn't have a winner. It was upsetting at the time, but racing has taught me to take defeat properly – something I never used to do,' said David. 'In retrospect, I must be satisfied with producing a horse to finish second in the Champion Hurdle, even if we had hoped to go one better. Months of planning went into that race, and he ran well . . . but just wasn't quite good enough to win. Much more than for myself, I was upset for the lads in the yard. They had been building themselves up for this day. I could not be seen to be too downhearted, however I felt inwardly. The trainer has to come back from such defeats with his head up high, get everyone working again, get the ship sailing towards the next big port.'

Scudamore found it hard to be so phlegmatic. Still young and at a stage in his career when defeat resembled disaster, he analysed every yard of the race and came to the conclusion that he had not done himself justice.

'I will always blame myself for the Champion Hurdle defeat. No matter how creditable it may be to have finished second, and how unexpected the eventual winner, I know I did not ride a good race on Broadsword.

'Perhaps I am being unfairly self-critical, but then that always has been part of my make-up. I never attempt to console myself after a defeat. My first instinct is always to wonder what I did wrong, and then to investigate until I find out.

139

'I honestly thought Broadsword would win. He was at his peak, the conditions were ideal and I had assessed that we had the beating of all the other fancied horses, from Ekbalco to Daring Run. It is hard to describe just how disappointed I felt that night, but it was certainly the most shattering day I have had in racing.

'Broadsword, I believe, had proved himself the best juvenile hurdler the previous season, despite being edged out in the Triumph Hurdle. I have a theory about that race, which is that it will generally be won by horses who need more than 2 miles. It is a very severe race for four-year-olds, with so many runners and invariably testing ground, and Broadsword put the record straight a few weeks later when he comfortably reversed placings with Baron Blakeney at Aintree.

'So now he had been aimed at the Champion. Only two five-year-olds had won the race in the previous fifteen seasons (Persian War was the other) and it would probably have been a more remarkable feat than we imagined at the time if he had achieved it. But, as the season progressed, Broady improved and finally we knew he was ready.

'That disappointing initial run at Newbury had been followed by a third, behind Heighlin and Ekbalco. At that stage we were not confident he would prove to be even worth running in the Champion, but in his next race, over 2½ miles at Cheltenham, he ran a blinder to win from Heighlin, Pollardstown and the rest of a very strong field.

'He had only one more race before the Festival – the City Trial Hurdle at Nottingham on a Monday in mid-February. It was not so much the winning of this event which gave us confidence, but the manner in which he won. Giving 20 pounds to Secret Ballot – who held the fastest-ever time for a 2-mile hurdle and went on to win the Royal Doulton at Haydock – Broadsword skated up by three lengths. It was an exhilarating feeling to be on board the horse that day. I knew then that we could win at Cheltenham.

'There is a lot of tension surrounding the Festival. As a relatively inexperienced jockey I think I still feel it much more severely than someone like John Francome, whose demeanour never seems to alter from meeting to meeting, big race or not.

'I had looked forward for weeks to Cheltenham and when it arrived I confess I was edgy. The Champion Hurdle was the highlight of the opening day and I know I was hard to talk to that morning. Marilyn wisely left me alone with my thoughts. It was not just plain nerves. I think I was more aware of what was to come, more caring about the outcome. I don't think a jockey can afford to have favourite horses as such, but Broadsword has always meant a great deal to me because he has been such a stepping-stone. Now, I wanted him to win for everyone concerned with the yard.

'If I went through the opposition once, I did it twenty times. Each time, despite the usual doubts and imponderables, I came up with the same answer. If Broadsword ran up to his best, he would beat them all. But there was a horse called For Auction, which even its Irish-based punters did not fancy, who was to make mugs of every one of us.

'I was intent on following my normal routine on the morning of the race. At the usual time I was up and about, ready to ride out at the Duke's yard. There was an unmistakable air of anticipation about the place. The lads could not help but discuss the horse's prospects and every one of them showed the loyalty one would expect from young blokes working with the animal and its connections for months beforehand.

'Superstitions do not bother me as they do some jockeys, but I had abided by a couple of quirky beliefs in the lead-up to the race. I refused to have any pictures of Broadsword taken in the current season displayed on the walls at home, because most racing pictures are of past or deceased stars; and I would not look up the prize money for the race. Small, silly things – but when a race means as much as this one did, nothing is too much trouble.

'Our race plan was much the same as it is every time Broadsword runs. He has to be ridden in a certain way, allowed to lob along for much of the race and then picked up for a final effort. He was no more than an ordinary horse on the flat and is not the quickest in a finish, but he jumps so superbly fluently that he can gain lengths at each obstacle when off the bridle. I knew he had to be properly positioned for that late burst, and I most feared the dazzling finishing speed of Ekbalco.

'It did not go entirely to plan. Donegal Prince led for the first half of the race, and as I began to make headway I was chopped more than once. Perhaps becoming impatient, Broadsword then switched himself on coming down the hill and I knew immediately it was too soon. By the sixth hurdle For Auction was ahead, and Broadsword was off the bridle and racing. I saw Ekbalco ranging upsides me on my outside and concentrated my attentions on seeing him off, subconsciously certain that For Auction would blow up on my inner. The next thing I knew, Ekbalco had been thwarted but For Auction had somehow sprinted eight lengths clear. I could hardly believe it, but from there it was impossible to win. All I could do was concentrate on ensuring second place.

'Neither David nor I said much afterwards. What was there to say? We had beaten all the obvious dangers, yet lost by seven lengths to one we had barely even considered. The fact that finishing second in a Champion Hurdle is a feat many trainers and jockeys would give a great deal for meant little to either of us at the time. I jumped down, talked the Duke and Lord Northampton, Broadsword's loyal owner, through the race, then went back to the weighing room to begin my private inquest.

'I had only one more ride that day, in the last race of the afternoon, and I did not linger afterwards. Cheltenham can be a very sociable meeting and many jockeys like to stay on afterwards, drinking and talking. I am afraid I was not in the mood for either. I went home in virtual silence and, I have to confess, I sulked the evening away, watching the video of the race time after time, and becoming steadily more depressed as For Auction kept going away from me.

'As the seasons go by and I mature as a racing person, I hope the pressure might not get to me quite so badly as it did last year. That race seemed the ultimate, and because I had lost it I was a failure. I could not get it out of my head, no matter how I tried, and inevitably I built the day, and the race, into something far more important than it really deserved. I grew more moody as the night progressed, and I am certain Marilyn must have been fed up with me. It is a habit I need to grow out of – it will make me a better person and probably a better jockey when I do.

'In the new light of the following morning I saw things slightly differently; Broadsword was only five, after all, and it was always bound to be a hard season for him. He would be stronger and more formidable in another twelve months, I was sure of that . . . and, on the same terms, I was equally convinced he would turn the tables on For Auction.

'Somehow I had to put all that behind me. The Festival was not only about the Champion Hurdle – there were two days to come, and I had nine booked rides in which to try to register my first winner at the meeting. Of those, uppermost in my mind were the two big events on the final day – the *Daily Express* Triumph Hurdle and the Gold Cup.

'The Triumph had caused me some agonized hours through the season, deciding between the habits and hopes of the better juveniles I had ridden. Eventually the Duke took the decision out of my hands and suggested I should ride Goldspun, which was the verdict I had independently reached anyway. Steve rode Lulav, our other contender, and John Francome had the ride on the favourite, Royal Vulcan, trained by Neville Callaghan, on whom we had alternated as riders through the season.

'On his best form, Goldspun had a very good chance, but the formbook hinted that his form had deteriorated since the bad weather. It proved to be the case, for although he came gamely to challenge the leaders two out, a mistake at the last put paid to all hope and we had to make do with eighth place behind the surprise winner, Shiny Copper, the third consecutive long shot to win this race.

'My mount in the Gold Cup was Captain John, for Michael Mouskos, and our starting price of 40–1 about summed up our chances. He is a nice horse but not quite in the class of Silver Buck, and I thought he ran a blinder to be sixth in severely taxing conditions.

'Apart from Broadsword, the Irish horse Chinrullah took me nearest to a winner, twice finishing second during the three days. But Cheltenham had passed me by again. Both David Nicholson and I were still awaiting our first success at the Festival, and still wondering whether Broadsword might make it third time lucky.'

The Grand National, Aintree

For many jump jockeys, and a good deal more National Hunt enthusiasts, Cheltenham is the *racing* highlight of the year, but Aintree is simply *the* highlight. The difference is that Cheltenham provides racing for the jumping connoisseur; the prize money is good in every event and any horse winning its race can justifiably be called the best in its particular class. Liverpool, with its ancient stands and ancient tradition, parades decent racing throughout its three days but is really only about one event, the perennially threatened national institution without which many people in Britain and around the world would know absolutely nothing about the jumping game. The National is often talked about in terms which suggest it is public property, yet the jockeys also feel both attached to it and inspired by it.

'I was only nine months old when my father won the Grand National,' Peter says, 'but it has probably influenced me for the rest of my life. Although I remember nothing of the ballyhoo in our part of the country after his success, I know just how much Liverpool meant to him in the years which followed, and how much he missed riding in the race when he was forced to pack up. I suspect I grew up believing that the first great ambition of a jockey should be to ride in the National, and the next should be to win it, and although day-to-day involvement with the sport as a business has led me

144

to modify my views slightly, there are still very few things I would rather do.

'The place has a magical atmosphere I have come to love, and although I am still a virtual novice, with only two rides in the race, it is something I look forward to throughout the season now. Naturally I want to win the race – I can scarcely imagine how I would feel in the hysterical atmosphere that always follows – but just to take part is an experience which can be compared with nothing else in racing. The whole nation knows the race is on, and it often seems that precious few are not interested.

'As soon as entries for the race are finalized and the weights published, the annual scramble begins. Trainers want a suitable jockey for their horse, or in some cases horses, and every jockey wants to ride something which has either a chance of winning or, at least, a chance of getting round. The National fences are stacked against you in any case, without riding something which struggles to get round at Newton Abbot or Fakenham.

'I was torn for weeks before the 1982 race. My options seemed to come down to three horses and each one had something to be said for him. The first, and probably the one I would most liked to have ridden if all things had been favourable, was Uncle Bing, trained by Richard Head at Lambourn. He had won the Topham Trophy, run over the National course, two years earlier and jumped like a stag under John Francome. I had a ride on him at Cheltenham early in the year and, although it was little more than a pipe-opener for the horse, he so impressed me that I immediately told Captain Head I would be available for the ride in the National if John was claimed by Fred Winter. I had never had a better ride over fences, and I honestly believed that if the horse stayed fit, he had every chance of winning the National.

'Then John Edwards, who trains just down the road from my father's place in Herefordshire, approached me to ride one of his entries, probably Again the Same. I rode the horse at Ascot towards the end of February. It was his first run of the season, yet he failed to win by

only half a length, despite giving a stone and a half to
Greenways, the only one to beat him. That too was a
strikingly good run, but a couple of weeks later he ran
again at Haydock and came back lame. There was
clearly some doubt about whether he would make it in
time for Aintree.

'By now I was riding regularly for David Morley, who
had a horse called Tragus entered. I won twice on him,
only small races at Fakenham and Folkestone, but he
jumped so brilliantly and won so well that I was swayed
more and more towards him as a National mount. With
the doubt over Again the Same's fitness, and continuing
confusion about whether or not John Francome would
be free for Uncle Bing, I opted for Tragus. Although we
were not even placed, it turned out to be the correct
decision.

'Every race at Liverpool builds to the climax of the
National. Although there are some good support events,
one of which gave me a winner on Silent Valley, they
are rather like the variety warm-up artists for Frank
Sinatra. Almost all conversation revolves around the
National, and the pubs and hotels of the Liverpool area
are dominated by the race.

'Although a lot of jockeys stay at the Holiday Inn and
plenty more at the old, traditional Royal Clifton up the
coast at Southport, I prefer to keep out of the heaviest
socializing and enjoy staying with our friends Michael
and Pat Sampson.

'I was up very early on the morning of the race,
determined to appreciate the day to the full. When I
was sixteen my father took me to Aintree and we went
to the course before breakfast to watch the horses work.
I remember staring at L'Escargot and thinking that he
looked so well. He seemed to sense that it was to be his
day, and of course it was.

'Tragus might not have been in L'Escargot's class but
he worked well that morning, and I enjoyed the atmosphere among the jockeys whose natural tension emerged
in a variety of ways, from overconfidence to joking pes-
simism. It was the same in the weighing room as the
minutes ticked away that afternoon. In one corner, John

Francome and Steve Smith Eccles were talking loudly
to each other through the nightmares to come and laugh-
ingly swopping gloom about their prospects of getting
round even one circuit, while Hywel Davies and I, both
less experienced and more intense, were optimistically
looking forward to riding a flashy finish after jumping
the last!

'It always takes a long time to get through the preliminary parade and the stewards' checking of horses
and equipment, and actually get the National started.
Butterflies churned around my stomach throughout this
period and I knew virtually everyone else down at the
start was feeling the same way. By the time the gate
went up I was as nervous as I've ever been, but also
elated at the same time.

'Most days, I don't notice the crowd. Very occasionally
when riding a finish I listen for the tell-tale roar which
indicates someone is looming upsides me, but otherwise
I block it out of my mind. At Aintree on National day
you can't help but notice. The roar, the motivating cres-
cendo of noise, makes you feel part of history.

'The horses hear it too, and that is not such good
news. They have in the main been trained with this one
race in mind, they are tuned up to a pitch and probably
will never feel stronger. Running to the first, they can
all too easily get carried away by the excitement of it all
and jump as if the problem was a mere park fence
instead of the unique Liverpool obstacle which demands
your getting close, and back on the horse's hocks. This
is why the first fence so often claims an unreasonable
share of casualties, which soared last year to ten; more
than 25 per cent of the field gone at the first.

'Tragus made a bad mistake there but survived, and
I was able to get him concentrating soon afterwards as
we left the din from the stands well behind and went out
into the country. Once settled, he began to jump really
well and my hopes soared again. I was nicely in touch
with the leaders, managing to avoid the frequent fallers
and those pulling up, of which Again the Same was one.
I started to think I had a genuine chance of getting
round, maybe even being placed.

'Halfway round the second circuit Tragus was still jumping well, the field had thinned dramatically and I was convinced we could be third. Grittar was clearly going best of all and looked most unlikely to be caught, and Anthony Webber on Hard Outlook still looked strong. I thought I could beat all the others.

'The race had taken more out of Tragus than I imagined. We lost ground four fences out and never regained our position. The horse had simply run out of puff and in any ordinary race I would have pulled him up. Probably I should have done so anyway, but in the National it is the last resort. If horse and rider have an ounce of energy left between them, it should be used, and somehow we completed the course in sixth place. Tragus finished very lame, although I had never felt him lose his action, and he had given me a super ride, one of my great thrills so far in racing.

'Of all the incidents during the race, probably the funniest occurred at Bechers. Approaching it for the second time, Hywel's mount Tiepolino was very tired and checked in front of the fence, not sure whether to jump or give up. John Francome was just behind on Rough and Tumble, an equally weary horse, who collided with Tiepolino's rear quarters, ejecting John into the thick undergrowth of Bechers. He had to extricate himself via the ditch, a humble pose for a champion.'

15

The End of a Dream

David Nicholson and Mike Scudamore happened to have spent the day of 26 April together. It was a Monday, late season, and the one race meeting, at Southwell, was of no interest to either of their stables, so they drove down to Wincanton to view some horses, prospective purchases for the future. Their business concluded, they were back in the car and on the road home when the sports news came on the radio and ruined a pleasant day for them both.

It was all uncomfortably vague. The presenter talked of a 'setback' to Peter Scudamore's bid for the jockeys' championship, and of a 'suspected' broken arm sustained in a fall at Southwell. A feeling of helplessness came over the two friends in the car.

Mike recalls, 'David and I looked at each other and said nothing for a bit. Then we consoled ourselves with the thought that nothing seemed to be definite, and maybe it was only a minor injury after all. It was a strange feeling, having news like that broken to you over the radio and I admit I just did not know what to do for a while. I wasn't shocked. You come to expect something like this now and again and I was hardened to it. But not knowing the full facts and having no immediate means of finding out – that was the worst thing.'

The clock in the homely kitchen of the Scudamores' house in Hoarwithy showed six o'clock. Mary was preparing something for Mike's return, wondering if he would be on time, and then wondering whether Peter had ridden a winner at Southwell that afternoon. He was now odds-on for the title after a brilliant month in which he had climbed twenty winners clear of John Francome. But Mary knew only too well that premature counting of chickens was a perilous pastime for racing folk. She wanted him to be champion, but she was at least equally concerned that he should complete the season in sound health.

She wandered through the passage to the lounge, deciding to use the Ceefax system to look up the afternoon's racing results. Standing beneath the two large paintings of Mike in his riding days, she pressed the buttons on the remote control unit until the racing page flashed up.

Above the Southwell results was the bald headline that Peter had been taken to hospital, his arm broken, after a fall. 'My first thought was, "Thank goodness it isn't something worse." I began to wonder which hospital he was in and then I felt dreadfully sorry for him. I knew how much the championship meant to him, you see, and now here was an injury, possibly denying him for the second successive year.'

Peter came round in the ambulance room, a small, functional cubbyhole in Southwell's rustic charm. He was shaken up, and he had been unconscious for some minutes. Slowly he began to reconstruct the episode.

'Everyone was saying I was home and dry, twenty winners ahead and only six weeks left. Break your leg tomorrow, they said, and John still won't be able to catch you. I had no wish to put that to the test, but nor was I convinced my lead was enough. I intended to carry on chasing winners right to the end, and that was why I went to Southwell for a ride in a novice chase.

'It had all been going so well. I had ridden forty-two winners in the previous eight weeks while John, who had suffered a little from illness and injury had managed only fourteen. The statisticians had told me that already I had beaten the record number of rides in a season; looking at my Peugeot spattered in mud, sweet papers on the floor and a permanently warm engine, I thought I had probably driven more miles than anyone else too. With about twenty-five racing days left the odds were against my challenging Jonjo O'Neill's amazing record of 149 winners in a season, but I meant to have a try.

'I had really begun to believe I would be champion at Chepstow on Easter Monday. It was one of the best jumping cards of the season, featuring the Welsh Champion Hurdle and the Panama Cigar Final, and I had a ride in each of the seven races – three each for the Duke and Mrs Rimell and one for Tim Forster. Not only was it a busy afternoon but potentially a successful one, as each of the seven horses had to be given some chance of winning on their best form. Nevertheless, that has been thought many times before and it was the sort of day on which two winners would have fully satisfied me.

'When I won the first two of the afternoon, all kinds of ambitions flicked through my mind. Going through the card was something which only a great optimist would consider, but there was no doubt that it could turn into my best-ever afternoon. John Francome won the third and Jonjo the fourth on Ekbalco, with Broadsword showing he had gone over the top for the year and only managing third place. But I then won the next two and went out for the last on the odds-on favourite, Palatinate. That one was disappointing, but I could hardly complain at having to settle for four! John had also ridden in every race but emerged with only one winner, a bonus for me, and the one disappointment of the day was that David's three runners happened to be the three on which I was beaten.

'It was a tremendous thrill, nicely topped off by news from the other courses. One of father's horses, True Lad, had won a novice chase at Wincanton, and Marilyn's brother Robert had ridden a first and second at Towcester – it represented a welcome change of luck for them both and added to the reasons for celebration. We did that in style, with a meal out for what seemed like dozens of people, supervised by the Duke and Broadsword's owner, Lord Northampton, at our local pub. I got home late and weary, but with that comfortable glow which comes with the end of all great days.

'Two weeks later I went to Southwell and the season ended, painfully and abruptly. I had been in Switzerland the previous day for a ride over hurdles, and chased up the motorway on the Monday morning. Southwell is not my favourite place, and the racing did not promise much, but with so much in my sights I was seeing every day as an exciting challenge, every race as a potential winner.

'To be a jump jockey you have to be a fatalist and accept that your number comes up for a fall and an injury now and again, and if you cannot actually plan the schedule of mishaps, at least you have a good idea that the average will work out around one fall every ten rides. But occasionally I curse myself because it seems it could have been avoided. Father always told me that on most occasions it is the rider's fault when he gets a horse on the floor, because he has been faced with a decision and has clearly got it wrong. It is certainly unusual to come back not knowing why you have fallen.

'In this instance my unreasonable annoyance stemmed from the fact that I had been offered two rides in the 2-mile handicap chase. One was a horse called Grand Trianon, for Sir Guy Cunard, the other Prairie Master, who had provided me with my second winner of the season way back in August. I chose the latter for no other reason than I knew him; I knew he had a chance and I was in the dark about Grand Trianon. I was to think again of that decision some months later, when I accepted the ride on Grand Trianon at the start of the 1982–83 season and he won first time out.

'There were a lot of runners in the race and staying out of trouble was difficult. The worst fence on the course is situated on the bend running away from the the stands, and it was there that I came to grief. The horse must have broken down badly in the final strides of approach because he just didn't take off an inch. I have a vivid memory of him ploughing straight into the roots of the obstacle, and of being shot a long way into the air. Then I knew no more until I found myself lying on a stretcher in the ambulance room.

'I knew immediately that the arm was broken. No one had to tell me. It had been put in a plastic splint, and as the incident presented itself in my mind again, I remember wondering if I would get back before the end of the season or whether, for the second successive year, the championship was to be decided by a fall.

'Being something of a coward, I probably expected to be in agony and I was surprised to find that the pain was not too severe, much more a nagging discomfort.

'In our job you grow accustomed to stretchers and hospitals; we probably see the inside of more hospitals than almost anyone else, and the enforced familiarity dispels any fear. My prime concern on sustaining an injury is simply to get the best treatment and to get it as quickly as possible – and that was what occupied my mind as I lay there waiting to be lifted into the ambulance.

'I was lucky. At Nottingham's main hospital I was seen by a doctor who recognized my name and knew a bit about the jockey's life. He contacted an orthopaedic specialist who agreed to operate that same night, and to my surprise I was told there would be no need for a plaster. The break was bad and the arm was to have two metal pins inserted to bind the fractures. Then it would be stitched up and left.

'When I woke up the following morning I felt much better if just a shade groggy, and I started to dwell on the championship again. The papers arrived and I spent an age staring at the card for the afternoon's meeting at Ascot. The usual high-class fields, the usual crop of good rides for J. Francome. I wondered what he was thinking that morning and how he meant to approach the rest of the season. Knowing him as I did, I suspected that my demise could just provide him with a spur to go flat out for every possible ride, and prove all those who had counted him out of the title race hopelessly wrong.'

John Francome had taken a day off on the Monday. Southwell never much appealed to him and he did not feel like scrambling for a poor ride which would boost the bank balance by £36 less petrol money, but might quite easily put him on the floor again. For weeks since his February fall at Newbury from Virgin Soldier, Francome had been below his cheery best. Twice he had told me conversationally that he would be prepared to pack up for the season and head for a recuperative spell in the sun, with only the odd game of tennis to exercise his weary body. But his lovely wife Miriam was away modelling in London, often confined to the city for week-long stays involving early starts and long hours. So, as they could not go away together, John resigned himself to labour on and booked his rides for the final Ascot meeting of the season.

He heard about Scudamore's injuries on the Monday night. It called for a revision of thinking. Even John himself had subconsciously accepted that he had lost the title, and if the loss hurt, well, he had recently not been sharp enough to worry too much. He looked through the racing calendar and totted up the number of remaining meetings at which he might be able to obtain rides. Twenty winners was a searching test at a time of year when most of the major stables were putting their horses away from the summer and only the firm-ground specialists were left, but he assessed that it was possible. It would take a lot of time on the telephone, very much longer in his car, and probably some frustrations on the course. But his mind was sharper, quite suddenly, with the new incentive.

Before going to Ascot on the Tuesday he made an important and controversial decision. If he somehow managed to ride twenty winners in the time available, and drew level with Scudamore at the top of the jockeys' table, he would retire for the season without a single ride more, thus ensuring a dead heat and a share of the jockey's title.

Although by no means confident that he would make up the leeway, Francome felt it only right that he should inform Peter of his plans. He telephoned Nottingham General Hospital, only to be told that Mr Scudamore was not yet well enough to accept phone calls. So he telephoned Mike Scudamore instead. 'If I ride twenty more winners,' he told the man for whom he had always had enormous respect, 'I will pack up for the year and Peter can share the championship. It would be the least I could do after the type of season he has had.'

154

At Ascot that afternoon Francome and David Nicholson met up outside the weighing room. The trainer, in his blunt and slightly wry manner, asked the champion how hard he intended to work for the rest of the season. Francome told him what he had decided.

'I was surprised, taken aback by him,' admitted Nicholson. 'On the one hand, I considered it would be a superb gesture, something which would show the true colours of National Hunt racing. But on the other hand, I confess I had my doubts whether he would carry it through. I could see all kinds of pitfalls for the plan – if he should ride the equalizing winner when he still had booked rides later one afternoon, for instance, what would he do? John asked me to tell Peter if he had not already heard from his father, but for a couple of days I said nothing. Then I did mention it to him, in a rather questioning voice. Scu's reaction was interesting. "If John says that is what he will do, then I believe he will do it." '

By the time David decided he would tell Peter of John's plan, the invalid jockey already knew. His father had been in to see him and had received the same reaction as the trainer.

Michael recalls, 'Mary and I went into the hospital the day after his operation and we were both surprised how well he was taking it all. I must say I expected a long face and few words, because he does get so intense about the job. But he was marvellous, quite cheerful and showing off the fact that he could actually move the arm already.

'I told him what John had said on the phone. I also told him that I believed him. By nature, I am a trusting sort, and I could not see any point in John going to the trouble of phoning me, of all people, if he did not mean to carry the thing through.

'Jockeys develop a regard for each other over the course of seasons spent together, and I think John genuinely respected the amount of work Peter had put into his efforts to be champion and did not want to deprive him purely on the strength of an injury.

'I didn't tell Peter, but I also thought John would

155

catch up. I know most people disagreed, and on paper the odds were against him doing it at the back end of a season. But he is a great jockey, and if he had the motivation – which clearly he did – I was pretty sure he would pull it off.

'That Friday night he rode a treble at Taunton, and then the writing was really on the wall.'

Peter was released from hospital on the Friday morning and told to take things easy at home, something he finds difficult at the best of times. Marilyn was surprised, however, by the equable nature of her husband patient. 'I expected him to stalk around the place, fretting about not riding and becoming grumpier by the day. In fact he acted as if he was quite relaxed.'

Scudamore explains, 'I was more philosophical in that position than I ever can be over losing a race I think I should have won. It was simply because I accepted there was nothing I could have done to prevent it, and that now there was nothing I could do to make the situation any better.'

While still in hospital, he had toyed with the idea of riding again before the end of the season. 'It was put in my mind by one of the doctors. I was fascinated by the fact that the injury did not need a plaster and it made me overoptimistic. I asked when I would be able to ride again, and they said I would be technically fit enough within a month. The word "technical" was operative, however, because although I would have had enough movement in the arm, another fall on it would have severely complicated matters. I teased myself more than anything, but when the Duke got to hear of it he was insistent that I put it out of my head.

'I can't pretend I cut myself off from racing, because that would have been completely against my nature. But I did not go to a jump meeting at all – standing there and watching, talking to my friends among the jockeys, would just have sharpened the feeling of being detached from it all, and I felt I was better off without that.

'*The Sporting Life* was still being delivered to the house every day, of course, and I looked through it to see what

156

John was riding and how he had done the previous day. I also studied David's runners and had the occasional twinge of regret that they were going racing without me, although in honesty he did not have many left running in the closing weeks. I was not missing very much.

'Once I was able to use the arm relatively normally, I even started enjoying the rest. And I shed some of the jockey's social restrictions I had grown accustomed to, started eating more and going out for a few glasses of wine in the evening.

'With Marilyn expecting our first child within a matter of weeks, it was an exciting time at home, and there was plenty of planning to keep me occupied. I was surprised to discover that even when my mind did stray to Worcester, Folkestone, Ludlow or wherever racing happened to be, I felt interested rather than aggravated.

'Everyone kept telling me that I was safe as champion, that John had no chance of catching me. But I had always believed he could, and as the days passed it became steadily more inevitable. When he finally drew level at Fontwell, there were four meetings remaining in the season. But he kept his word, as I always knew he would.

'I saw John a few days later. It was a warm summer's day, the first Friday of June. I had spent the morning at the Oval, watching the one-day cricket international, then had to dash down to Epsom to meet John and do a television interview with him over the sharing of the championship. It annoyed me that various writers and broadcasters had already been openly critical of what John had done and accused him of cheating the people who had backed him to be champion. But when the question was raised by Brough Scott, he gave a typically blunt answer.'

'I told everyone who asked that I had just done what I thought was right, and I really didn't care too much what other people thought,' said Francome. 'I had to work bloody hard to catch up with Scu, and maybe the toughest of professionals will say I should have carried on, because it could just as easily have been me in hospital with a broken arm. But this is still a sport, and Pete had done so much through the season. I had been champion before; it was new to him, and he deserved to have something to show for riding 120 winners.'

It seems probable that Francome was spurred on by his own statements. Having told Peter and his close connections that he would share the title, he also let it be known to the racing press. It made a good news story and every paper used it. Francome had now not only ensured that he could not change his mind – in the improbable event of it occurring to him to do so – but had also set himself a target in the most public fashion. He then set out to achieve it and, in succeeding, dragged himself to courses he had never even visited before.

The climax of his travels was daunting even to think about. He rode at an evening meeting at Taunton, Somerset, on Thursday, 27 May. The following day, extremely early, he set off from his Lambourn home to Sedgefield, just off the A1 on Teesside. Despite his dislike of spending any nights away from home – in the past he has often driven back to Lambourn each night of the Aintree Grand National meeting rather than stay in a hotel – Francome had accepted rides at Cartmel, in Cumbria, for Saturday afternoon so he stayed with a northern jockey on Friday night and drove across country the next morning. Then, after riding a winner in Cartmel, he jumped back into his Renault for a 200-mile motorway dash to Southwell, near Nottingham, and a ride in the evening meeting.

'By the time I reached home that night I had driven more than 800 miles in forty-eight hours and I was knackered,' he confirmed. 'I had been to Sedgefield once or twice before, but never to Cartmel. I also never realized just what a different way of life the northern jockeys lead. They might have got me drunk,' he grinned, the mocking complaint of a man who seldom drank anything stronger than half a pint of lager until he developed the taste for an occasional Scotch this year.

That cluttered weekend settled the fate of the championship. Francome came through it with body and soul intact, if weary, and with enough winners in the bank to know he would need a disastrous last week to rob him of the one more he needed.

'I rode horses during that last fortnight that I would never want to get on again,' he said. 'One of them won, but scared me so much they would need to pay me a fortune to persuade me to ride the thing once more. But it was another winner, and I reached the stage where I was going anywhere and riding anything for one of them.'

It scarcely caused a ripple when Francome finally drew level and quit. One of the great sporting contests of recent years had been honourably settled, and both John Francome and Peter Scudamore could call themselves the champion. Some still expressed regret about Francome's actions, most applauded the generous spirit behind it. But in the cosy stone houses at Hoarwithy and Condicote there were still shades of sadness.

Mary, for her part, became more involved in the pursuit than she would care to admit. But she did it her own way, rather as she refuses to watch some of Peter's races but cares passionately about the outcome. 'It was quite simple,' explained Michael. 'For three weeks, she would not open *The Sporting Life*. She tried to cut herself off from what John was riding. But she knew, really. . . .'

At Cotswold House David Nicholson's season came to a quiet close. It had been his most successful ever – fifth place in the trainers' table behind the likes of Dickinson, Winter, Gifford and Walwyn, and almost £130,000 earned from fifty-seven winners, the vast majority ridden by Peter Scudamore.

'I wanted him to be champion. In fact I was very eager that it should happen and not just for him, though God knows he deserved to get something from the season. I wanted him to win it for his parents, who are wonderful people, and, yes, for everyone here in my yard. For me, too. It would have been a feather in all our caps, after all. As it is, everyone will still call him the champion – but I think both he and John would like it to be clear-cut next year.'